Obama Music

Some Notes From A South Sider Abroad

Bonnie Greer

Legend ▌Press
Independent Book Publisher

Legend Press Ltd, 3rd Floor, Unicorn House,
221-222 Shoreditch High Street, London E1 6PJ
info@legend-paperbooks.co.uk
www.legendpress.co.uk

British Library Cataloguing in Publication Data available.

ISBN 978-1-9065582-4-6

Set in Times

Printed by JF Print Ltd., Sparkford.

Cover designed by Keira Rathbone
www.keirarathbone.com

Legend **Press**

Independent Book Publisher

To my deeply missed late father, my uncles, my brothers, my brothers-in-law, my male cousins and nephews and great nephews, to my husband, and to all those men who have been and still are brothers and fathers, friends, and other good and kind things to me…and to the old brother with the cane on Michigan Avenue, Chicago, who told me to go ahead and do my book.

Acknowledgements

American Sermons: The Pilgrims to Martin Luther King Jr. Michael Warner Books.

The Audacity Of Hope, Barack Obama, Crown Publishers, New York, 2006

Dreams From My Father, Barack Obama, Canongate, 2007

Renegade – The Making Of the President, Richard Wolffe, Crown Publishers, New York, 2009

Obama: From Promise To Power, David Mendell, Amistad/Harper Collins 2008

Michelle – A Biography, Liza Mundy-Pocket, Star Books/Simon Schuster, 2008

Michelle Obama – First Lady Of Hope, Elizabeth Lightfoot, The Lyons Press/The Globe Pequot Press, 2008

Considering Genius, Stanley Crouch, Basic Civitas Books/ Perseus, 2006

Prologue

I was born and raised on the South Side. It has a particular musical landscape and history that helps to fill in part of the picture that is the 44th President of the United States.

To understand, at a deeper level, the phenomenon that is Barack Obama, it is necessary to know something about the community that he made his base, where his wife and children were born and raised, where he began his career and where his private home is located: the South Side of Chicago.

Obama Music is a mixture of tales of my own life growing up on the South Side, mixed in with stories and observations about Obama, linking all of this in with the music, the musicians and the music scene, beginning in the past and moving forward. Obama writes in *The Audacity Of Hope:* 'I've always felt a curious relationship to the sixties. I'm a pure product of that era...'

And so am I.

Now, *Obama Music* is made up of all kinds of music: hip hop; country, classical, rock and roll, all of which were heard on Inauguration Day.

But it is also the blues, gospel, soul and jazz, especially from the golden eras; when the people of the South Side began to build the great institutions, and the great solidarity, that enabled Barack Obama to become the most powerful person on the planet.

Living away from the place you were born, living 'abroad', sometimes means that you get the details badly wrong.

I wrote in *The Guardian* at the beginning of Obama's Presidential campaign:

'The truth is that I just can't warm to Obama.

'Maybe I'm just too working-class, too old-school, to trust black people who look that slick, outside of show business or the church. Maybe I distrust someone who allows others to compare him to JFK or even MLK. I was around when they were alive. He's not them.'

This book will show you how I moved from there, to this point in *The Telegraph* at the end of his campaign:

'In his triumphant election campaign of 1984, Ronald Reagan declared: "It's morning in America." If that is the case, then the election of Barack Obama as the 44th President of the United States, and the first African-American to hold that awesome office, represents high noon, the moment at which the light is at its brightest and strongest. America has stepped away from its robust, too often reckless and romantic youth into maturity.'

But living abroad, being an expat, can make you so out of it that you have a kind of analogue edge.

Sometimes you can see bigger shapes, deeper patterns.

You use old-fashioned, maybe even 'incorrect' words and ways of looking at things because they better describe how you feel, what you mean.

I use the word the word 'black' in this book instead of 'Black' or 'African American' because for me 'black' speaks of triumph and perseverance, it links me to my rural ancestors and to the

South Side and the time that I grew up in.

It is the word that Barack Obama uses most often to describe himself.

I can see from my vantage point across the ocean that being born black in America at the beginning of 1964, having intelligence and energy, the support and encouragement of a loving, supportive, and hard working family was a very lucky thing.

This is because 1964 was arguably the most important date in black American history since the Emancipation Proclamation in 1863.

Michelle Obama was born in January, 1964 and these are just a few of the things that happened during her first year of life: when she was two months old, Malcolm X and Martin Luther King met for the first and last time, signalling a major shift in the Civil Rights Movement; when she was six months old, President Lyndon Baines Johnson signed the 1964 Civil Rights Act effectively beginning the process of ending segregation and ushering in other measures like Affirmative Action, paving the way for bright black kids to attend elite universities.

1964 was the year that Nelson Mandela made his defiant speech before being sentenced to prison, sending the anti-apartheid movement to another level.

A month before Michelle's first birthday, Martin Luther King was awarded the Nobel Peace Prize.

Oh, and 1964 was the year that Dionne Warwick had one of her greatest hits: *You'll Never Get To Heaven If You Break My Heart*. A big breakthrough for her.

It becomes clearer and clearer to me as time passes that jazz and soul are hybrids. They are the complex, urbanized offshoots of blues and even gospel. And because they are hybrids they are 'open systems' able to influence easily other kinds of music while they themselves are open to change.

From my perspective, jazz and soul are also responses to electrification and the experience of the city. Their open systems make them fluid, malleable, forever mutating into genres and portals such as hip-hop.

This is a South Side Presidency.

It is about the music of that train that brought my people up from the South to the South Side. They brought with them their blues, their gospel, soul and jazz. They deepened these musics, thereby changing not only themselves but the city and the nation and the world.

They are reflected in a poem, copied down by Zora Neale Hurston, the great Harlem Renaissance writer, from a sermon she heard at the end of the 20's.

I heard the whistle of the damnation train
Dat pulled out from the Garden of Eden loaded wid cargo
goin' to hell
Ran at break-neck speed all de way thru de law
All de way thru de prophetic age
All de way thru de reign of kings and judges
Plowed her way thru de Jordan
And on her way to Calvary when she blew for de switch
Jesus stood out on her track like a rough-backed mountain
And she threw her cow-catcher in
His side and His blood ditched de train.
He died for our sins.
Wounded in the house of his friends.

Everybody has their own *Obama Music*.
This is mine.

THE BLUES

If My Hands Could Get What My Eyes Can See

Slipping, Sliding, Tones

There is a moment in *The Audacity Of Hope* when Obama is questioning his very essence: his restlessness, his need to keep moving.

The question I ask is this: had he been attracted to Chicago because of this restlessness, this desire to keep moving?

Chicago has always been a centre of transport, of moving.

One of its nick-names is 'The Go'.

The railroads were and are in Chicago because it was and is still considered to be the crossroads of the country.

Massive interstate highways cut right through.

Chicago has itchy feet.

Like the blues.

His chief advisor at the White House has stated that the President likes to slip out and walk around a bit, be on his own.

To my mind, that natural restlessness, that need to break out, is the essence of the blues.

The blues are said to have a 'slippin', slidin' tone.'

The improvisation beneath the careful exterior.

'If my hands could get what my eyes can see,' the great Chicago bluesman Lonnie Brooks sings in *Eyeballin'*.

'Eyeballin' – the refusal to look down when your 'better' is speaking to you; the 'yes, we can' to fate and the way things seem to be – is what embodies the Chicago brand of the blues, and the South Side itself.

'Eyeballin' invites re-creation. Looking someone in the eye can enable you to see yourself.

It is said that the President is pre-occupied with how others see him.

'Eyeballin' lets you see the reflection in someone else's gaze.

If you can do this, then you can get busy.

You can improvise. Re-make.

Obama set out to get what his eyes could see.

Obama feels this as a constant process on the South Side.

Chicago is his place.

Check it out:

There are numerous bluesmen who called themselves 'Son', 'Guitar'. This is not an act of plagiarism or ripping off somebody's else's act (although some might have done it for that reason, that's for sure), but to 'name' that part of them that had to move on, that had to believe in the vision that they had seen on that crossroads where they first took up the blues.

Obama writes of several crossroads in his life.

The notion of the crossroads is integral to the blues, and to the Chicago blues.

The Devil At The Crossroads

The crossroads is a Yoruba concept, from the Yoruba people of Nigeria, cousins of the Africans in the New World.

It is believed that at the crossroads, usually in a heavily wooded area, there lies in wait the Yoruba god or orisha Elegba, the Trckster, or the Devil to Christians.

You could be just walking along, minding your business, and step on what you think is a rock, and suddenly a laugh emanates from it. It is Elegba.

Elegba, the Trickster, usually has something in store.

Or, he can grant a wish.

You can hear Elegba lurking in the ice-cold, death-confronting blues of Robert Johnson.

You can hear him in the archetypal character of 'Jody', the guy who slips into your house and takes your place in bed next to your wife while you're at work doing something back-breaking and demeaning and soul-destroying.

He is one of the faces of Elegba.

Above all, the orishas simply appear, shaking the dust off their feet and set about their work.

You can justify what is happening to you when one appears. You can call it madness; hallucinations; luck; fate.

But even the most rational among us have to stop for a minute and ask ourselves if an orisha is amongst us and exactly who it might be.

Because it is possible that it was the orishas who kept us alive, and who, from time to time, show themselves in human form.

And they are always present in the blues

You can cross into gospel-land and pray to Jesus but when an orisha makes itself known, you can't justify it, even to the Lord.

You can call it madness, hallucinations, luck, fate; getting 'happy' and suddenly jumping up in church and 'talking in tongues'. You can go into 'testifying' – a sometimes made up on the spot rambling monologue.

'Testifying' would bear witness to your truth.

Much of classic soul has a blues underpinning, but overtly takes a page out of the gospel playbook and often lets the lead singer 'testify.'

(Listen to the exquisite lead singer of The Four Tops – Levi Stubbs – as he steps off into his own zone of testifying, leaving the world behind during his solo riff on that soaring hymn to unrequited love: *Bernadette*.

There is many a Mississippi legend from down in the part of the state that my father and his people come from, in which a not-so-great guitarist goes into the woods and comes out a virtuoso.

They would say that 'he done met the devil at the crossroads'. Elegba.

You have to watch out.

You can play like the devil – sublimely – but you sometimes have to pay for it.

The immortal Robert Johnson sings of the 'hellhound on my

trail', and he was found poisoned to death, some say in payment to that very hellhound that gave him the gift of the blues.

Who is to say?

Traditional blues is not about analyses and codification. It is about signs and portents, deeply felt emotion plainly spoken; forbidden sex; doomed love; intuition; chance; and a world without the God you were given when they threw you off the boat after the Middle Passage.

Pretty frightening stuff at the high tables of the West.

The real blues is about feeling when to come in, feeling when to do it.

The Delta blues – named after that region of the state of Mississippi located on the delta of the Mississippi River, one of the ancestral homes of South Siders – is father of the Chicago blues sound.

This Chicago blues sound would have permeated all of the places Obama worked and lived in, saturating what many would have seen as his rather laid-back West Coast-Honolulu ambiance.

Twelve-bar blues would have knocked the ukulele for six.

At first, twelve-bar existed only in the playing and the feeling of those who sang it and heard it and lived it.

Later, like everything natural, it came to be written down, its elements codified, books came into being; orchestras took it up; sects developed.

It became accessible to outsiders. Then it became 'respectable'.

But no matter what, feeling is always there in the blues.

This feeling could be first heard in what were once called 'race records'.

Race records were a product of the rigid segregation of American society.

They were marketed exclusively to the black community, had their own stars and charts, existed in their own world.

Black people brought the records with them to the North.

In a strange way this very musical segregation, part of the general apartheid was made useful. This is the Entropic way, that way in which negative or seemingly useless energy is used and forged into something strong and positive, bristling with power and the power of change.

It was used to create institutions, philosophies, approaches to religion and culture and education and government that created networks and alliances.

Inner fortresses were built, full of pride and direction and focus that made something whole and of itself.

This Something could, in time, have the power to make a black man mayor of one of the most segregated cities in the US.

This Something could give the world the most powerful person on earth.

It could.

And it did.

King Bee

Look at this for a minute:

See the faded sepia colour of Okey Records' 'Race Records' covers with the photograph of the guitar-guy, a very anthropological-looking cover, his happy grin and jaunty air guaranteed to bring only good memories of back home; see the dirty-orange coloured cover of Victor Records with the line drawing of the black man and the guitar – very 'authentic' and melancholy – the man sitting down, his back against a sack of something, his head back.

Check it.

Don't you get the feeling that he is 'hobo-ing': riding the rails illegally, moving toward freedom, and the hell with the consequences? Kind of. Because nobody wants to die. Not really. Who knows what's on the other side?

If there is another side.

See the subtitles: 'vocal blues', 'spirituals', 'red hot dance tunes', 'sermons', 'novelties'.

Billboard Magazine published 'race records' charts between the years 1945 and 1949, starting with what was played on various juke box 'plays'. From 1948 it included a record of the sales from those juke boxes.

All of the great blues musicians and vocalists – everyone you would have ever heard of – would have been marketed under the 'race record' label. And paid accordingly.

No prizes for guessing that the words 'blues artist' and 'rich ' do not exist in the same sentence, except if that sentence also includes the name of the record label that gathered the profits!

Blues men and women plied their trade up and down the 'chitlin' circuit', a touring route of halls and clubs, bars and cheap motels where you could spend the night, because there were no places on the road where black people were allowed to stay except where they owned their own.

Chitlins' are chitterlings, a delicacy made from the entrails of the pig (poor folks made food out of every last part of an animal), that our father used to boil slowly in a large pot on Sundays, and whose smell drove me far away from the house whenever it was bubbling away, but which (served with a particularly piquant hot sauce) was Daddy's Numero Uno comfort food and Sunday afternoon's *raison d'etre*.

In other words, 'chitlin'' means down-home-no-bullshit-you'd-better-know-how-to-play/sing. This ensured that the circuit was vibrant, and a real testing ground.

That line in *New York, New York*: 'If you can make it there, you can make it anywhere' was understood by anyone who stepped up on a stage and survived.

Chicago's South Side with its majestic Regal Theatre was one of the capitals of the circuit, one more reason for musicians to head north, confident that Nirvana awaited.

My mother (whose middle name she only recently deigned to tell us, very typical of black Southerners of a certain vintage who seldom let anyone know their real name for fear of a hoodoo whipped up against them, by an enemy using their full name as a key to the curse!) was born in Nashville, Tennessee, but grew up in Chicago.

A city girl through and through.

Our late father, however, had fled in his teens out of the depths of Mississippi where he had had the unfortunate and potentially fatal habit of speaking his mind too often and too forcefully to white people for him to remain where he was born and hope for a long and peaceful existence in this world.

He also brought his music to Chicago, because, after all, what was the point of it all without books and music, and in time a good woman and a family of your own?

I can recall the '45's and '78's that he had collected, the names of the musicians are like the list that Shakespeare gives Henry V to recite in that rousing St Crispin's Day speech: Big Walter; Howlin' Wolf; Magic Sam – King Of West Side Blues (behind Muddy's Emperor); the great Otis Rush; Luther Johnson (Guitar Junior); Sunnyland Slim.

Dad's books included those of that late, great Chicago chronicler of the common people, Studs Terkel which he would read while listening to the immortal Otis Spann, Sonny Boy Williamson, and James Cotton.

And Bo Diddley.

Everything has been said about Bo Diddley, including how his revolutionary riff has been ripped off – I mean borrowed or one of my favourite words: 'hommaged' – on numerous occasions without acknowledgment; his songs recorded by the likes of: Elvis Presley, Buddy Holly, The Stones, The Who, Springsteen, U2, The Jesus and Mary Chain, the Smiths, Eric Clapton, George Michael, Elton John, David Bowie, The Police, The White Stripes, the

Clash, and Black Eyed Peas, plus loads of descendants of these bands who probably don't know they're even channelling Bo Diddley.

Can I say that they don't know 'Diddley' as we say on the South Side (and probably everywhere else), a statement of the highest stage of ignorance.

But for me, well those early blues days are all about 'Slim Harpo'.

I don't know why, but the name 'Slim Harpo' still puts dread in my heart and a chill down my spine, a frisson runs through me like ice.

I first heard that name as a little child when my parents were talking about something I wasn't supposed to be listening to.

And, being a very curious, even nosey kid, I didn't go away, but kept saying over and over in my mind: 'Slim Harpo, Slim Harpo, Slim Harpo'.

Slim Harpo.

This was the stage name of James Moore, his last name after the word 'harp', slang for the blues harmonica.

His name and his music evoke in me all of the terror of the Mississippi woods where a black person could meet his true love or the Ku Klux Klan, both within seconds of one another.

This primal terror, with its accompanying reticence and outright 'clamming up' is in the bones of South Siders, making some of them not actually say anything of real use while all the while talking away a mile a minute.

You can walk away from a South Sider and realize after a few minutes that they were, in the immortal words of one of James Brown's songs: 'Talkin ' Loud and Sayin' Nothin''

Folks are polite, but distant. And they neither talk to nor pay attention to strangers.

Which is why, when I was a critic and I got word that someone was angry with something I had said on air or had written, I would be perplexed.

I was a stranger to them.

What did what I have to say really matter?

Slim Harpo would have laughed

Finally, the great day arrived when I got to hear my dad's crackly record with the yellow label Slim Harpo's the immortal *King Bee*.

You can hear it yourself on You Tube.

It still gets to me.

As far as I'm concerned you can forget The Rolling Stones' version on their first album; likewise The Floyd, The Doors, The Dead, and especially John Belushi's piss-take. Kick them all to the kerb.

Listen to Harpo himself, a true Devil's-Son-In-Law, the highest accolade that can be attributed to any male blues musician (don't know what the female equivalent of this could be…)

Listen:

First comes that stomping blues guitar, hard and dark like the Mississippi woods.

Then Slim arrives, sounding like a malevolent bee:

'Yeah, well I'm a king bee, buzzin' around your hive…'

He goes into his riff on the wings of: 'well, buzz awhile; sting it then…' and the guitar pings with a kind of an acidity, very, very spare and silvery, and after that Harpo implores the women all over the world to become his Queen Bee.

A dubious invitation especially when he plays his harp like a siren.

It all ends with old Harpo, malevolent like the guy who's going to take all of your stuff and I don't mean your packet of crisps singing the way a cobra must sound: 'I can buzz all night long.'

There he is, ladies and gentlemen, especially the ladies: Slim Harpo, slim as a knife blade, skin as black as two in the morning in a blackout; looking like he's seen things that he cannot say, but can certainly sing about, Slim Harpo is the man your mother warned you about; the guy you bump into in a bar and decide to runaway with; the one who doesn't give a hang about anything, and mostly that includes you.

After all, hypocrisy is his enemy.

Slim's blues are not for the faint-hearted.

They are the Way Of The Cross – and with Slim Harpo, it's you who carries the cross.

South Side doom and desire is a long way from the beaches of Waikiki.

The Name

From time to time, television likes to dig up old footage of Obama – 'At The Beginning':

There is a restaurant review (!) that he did that aired once on a local station in Chicago.

From what I can recall he is talking about a local restaurant – soul food, I think – with all of the elevated dinner party chatter expertise that we sometimes displayed on *Newsnight Review*, in other words, not exactly expert but relatively harmless and fleetingly entertaining in that everybody-has-a-right-to-have-a-go pseudo democratic spirit.

One of my favourite 'At The Beginning's is of the future President somewhere – it looks like backstage at a convention-standing pretty forlornly, while a reporter is writing impatiently on a small white pad what Obama is spelling out for him: 'B-a-r-a-c-k-O-b-a-m-a'.

Obama is leaning into the reporter, checking that his name is spelled correctly After that he assists the reporter in pronouncing his name.

The poor reporter can't get his head around it.

Obama repeats his name slowly.

Finally the reporter gets it right. There's a look of triumph on his face.

Obama flashes that million dollar smile.

Good, isn't it?

The first time I ever heard the name 'Barack Obama' was while walking down Greek Street in Soho on a rainy Wednesday after-noon in the autumn of 2006. I was with Alan, a friend from Boston, Mass.

I was helping to put together – for the following spring – a two hundredth anniversary commemoration of the Abolition Act for the British Museum, and was mentioning the need for another speaker as Alan was busily telling me about his flat in Mayfair.

Sometimes I think that there must be some kind of scam aimed at New York, LA, and Chicago in which Americans are lured to London and told that they will be living in Mayfair, when they are really being rented places on the edge of Soho, or Islington.

Which was my friend Alan's situation: living in Soho and trying to convince me that the apartment we were both standing outside of on Greek Street was located near Hyde Park.

To get him off that tack, I wondered aloud who we could get from America to keynote the event at the BM.

Suddenly he mentioned a friend who was on secondment from Harvard Law and interning in the Commons – which he had found to be a strange and dizzying mixture of shambolic and ruthlessly efficient (in the backstabbing and pub-crawling-after-work) departments.

He texted the friend who got back to him right away with a name: 'Barack Obama. Great spkr.'

Who was that?

Alan explained that his friend was a member of an association called the Black Law Students Association Alumni or something like that at Harvard and Obama was pretty active in that so everybody kept in touch.

And oh, yeah, Obama happened to be the junior senator from the state of Illinois.

My home state!

I blurted out: "Illinois elected somebody called …. 'Barack Obama'!"

Because, frankly, I didn't buy the name.

Back in the day, when I was growing up on the South Side, it was the fashion for us young bloods to adopt African names, or names that sounded African to us.

Well, a famous hair oil company based in Chicago – 'Afro Sheen' – had a commercial then with the jingle: 'Wazu, wazuri, use Afro Sheen.'

If they could say that, we could rename ourselves.

Some people went the whole nine yards, came up with these names and insisted that they be called by nothing else.

Their old 'slave name' was dead and buried.

It didn't matter if their old name had been the name of a beloved matriarch or patriarch, or someone who had held the family together through thick and thin.

It was gone with the wind. *Verboten*. *Fini*.

Courteous little boys I had known from primary school, neat and eager in their little suits and bow ties, had become dashiki-wearing spouters of 'New Africa Speak' with names a yard long and attitudes to match.

A handful of them cobbled together a few half-understood tenets of Islam and Judaism and used this new philosophy to basically amass a lot of women under one roof, and under their control, along with getting loads of money from followers who were sick and tired of white folks oppressing them.

They were ready for some good old black oppression!

"At least he's a brother," one of my high-school friends explained as she disappeared into a commune further South, under the direction of an ex-altar boy who, when we were kids, everyone had tipped for the priesthood.

'At-least-he's-a-brother' had done more than his bit to go forth and multiply. He had dozens of kids, and soon my friend ceased speaking to me, ceased speaking altogether to anyone who had anything to do with white people.

I had tried to explain that I did not actually know the Italian guy who collected the rubbish from outside my flat on campus, but that cut no ice with my former friend, or her cult.

My mission was to get somebody black to do the job and run the white guy off the block.

Then I did toy with the idea of changing my name.

I had had my right nostril pierced and wore seven earrings – three on my left lobe and four on my right – so what was a name change?

Besides, I had wanted to demonstrate my 'consciousness', show that I was part of the new movement sweeping all of us young people along, a movement which rejected the Martin Luther King ethos – at least what we knew of it – to embrace the ethos of Malcolm X (what we knew of that).

I silently called myself 'Abena', an Akan name from Ghana which means 'woman born on Tuesday.'

I stress that I called myself this silently.

My parents would have laughed to death if I'd tried to change my name to something African.

My devotedly Royalist mommy had named me after Prince Charles.

So what more could I want?

The name 'Bonnie' as in 'Bonnie Prince Charlie' was what the new royal baby was being called in the newspapers, and by naming me after him, my mother felt that she could be a part of the party.

She had truly hated – she told me once – that the word 'negro' had been stamped on my birth certificate.

I wasn't a 'negro', or anything except her daughter, her first child.

She had wanted it off.

My father, who had seen Dachau shortly after its liberation, had told her that he had seen the word and had hated it, too, but had seen worse.

Much. Much worse.

Mamma fell so sick that she had had to go to hospital.

The combination of the cold house that the three of us shared with other families in extremely cramped conditions, with very little privacy; plus her new duties involving a newborn in such a cramped space with an overbearing landlady who kept all of the doors closed, soon sent her there with a case of pneumonia when I was a few months old.

I know that you can't recall anything before one year of age – the most common age when memory develops is three – but at any rate, the separation from my mother must have been so traumatic to me that I can recall snapshots from that time. My grandmother's room, small, with soft light; she darker than my mother, closer to my father's complexion. My mother, big-eyed and fragile, clad in a bright yellow bed jacket with a ribbon hanging from her neck, propped up in bed; the smell of the room which was comforting to me.

We had had no choice but to live where we did.

Housing was restricted for black people on the South Side then.

I was recalling all this as I stood in that Soho street all those years later.

We met Alan's friend the next day.

He explained excitedly that Obama had been the first African American President of the *Harvard Law Review*, the most prestigious law journal in the country, and had always maintained a keen interest in his fellow black alumni, as well as the students, etc.

It all sounded good but I just couldn't accept The Name…

I mean, this had to be some brother named Alvin Jones – great name, by the way, I'm just making a point here – who had changed his daddy's name to…. 'Barack Obama.'

Then the friend showed us a photo that he carried with him, of Obama, and himself.

I thought that there was something just too smiley, too fey, too 'corporate', too 'buppie', too un-'regular' about this 'Obama' guy.

At any rate, Alan's friend had a hotline to him and was sure that he could get him over to take part in the ceremony.

He was my senator, after all, and I was kind of enthusiastic about that. Somebody to shoot the breeze about Chicago with during the speeches.

Lots of work was done to make it happen.

And it almost did.

Obama's office was kind and responded to everything, but in the end, the decision was made that it was best that he stay in the

US for the moment.

I thought it was sad that he couldn't make it, nothing more.

But Alan kept saying to me, over and over, that his friend really rated Obama and that I had to get on board the love train because it was leaving the station.

I just didn't get it.

Too far away.

When Alan got back to Boston, Mass. he sent me a copy of *Audacity*, but I just put it on the shelf.

Alan said that Obama was going to run for President.

Come on, the guy looked super-vain, hardly 'regular'; hardly 'down'; more like some Abercrombie and Fitch ad.

Ralph Lauren, I decided, must be after him.

In other words, this was not someone who could be seriously considered for the Presidency. This was NOT the first BLACK President.

The first black President was going to look like Sidney Poitier or Denzel Washington. Or some blues musician like Son Seal or Otis Clay – hard, clued-up, 'bad'.

And this 'Obama' had created a father who had been an African intellectual, too?

Right.

Besides, 'Obama' had to have an attitude, taking such a pretty elegant African name. He had to have chosen this name because he knew that once upon a time, even in the bad old days, a white person could walk into a white Southern church accompanied by an African in full regalia and that would be ok.

But if he brought the black guy from down the road, they could be both swinging in the wind after sundown.

You had to be the blues to be the African American President.

Especially if you're talking about coming from the South Side.

I was clear about that.

The Summer of '08

I came back to Chicago for the first time in three years to represent the British Museum at the opening of the Benin Exhibition. At the Art Institute of Chicago.

We stayed near the Art Institute of Chicago, in the Loop, and on the surface, I had never seen the city more glorious.

It was summer and the living was easy.

For some.

The day after I arrived, I took a taxi home to the South Side.

The sprawling housing estates that had practically straddled the expressway were gone. They had been buildings so huge and all-encompassing that they were simply impossible to explain to a European.

Inside they were everything a dismal sink estate was here in Britain but multiply that by stories, and numbers of people, and misery.

In Britain there is no culture of the summer fire-hydrant display.

You'd open a hydrant on a blazing summer's day so that people could cool off.

In the bad old days, if you ventured down to the lake front you could be attacked by white gangs…and killed.

If you were black you followed that old admonition and 'stayed back', and at sundown, if you were a little kid, you sat in your wet underwear – the only bathing costume most folks could afford – and listened to somebody pick out the blues on a guitar or a harmonica.

The blues was Chicago style, electrified and naughty and wry.

As a kid you could not understand the nuance, the innuendo, the double entendre, which – like Calypso – can be a devastating comment on the times.

What you did was sit in the wet and listen to old folks sing and something inside you knew that the base of this singing was loss and yearning, but for what you could not be sure.

Swimming was not an activity black people excelled at because, traditionally, we were denied access to the beaches and the public pools. But my sister's husband managed to become a champion swimmer back in Nebraska, teaching black folks at the public pool reserved for them and known as 'the inkwell.'

My California nieces and nephews are hearty surfers.

Never thought we would have swimmers in our family.

Our mother had been too frightened to take us regularly to the beach.

That summer, as we came off the highway near the little red bungalow where my six brothers and sisters and I grew up, the house where my father died, and which my mother still occupies, I saw an old lady – and I mean old – standing on the side of the street, selling small bottles of water.

The blues were crackling out of an old radio that she had at her feet.

Vietnam vets were at the exit of the highway, begging for handouts. Other guys who should have been enjoying their retirement ran up to cars offering to wash the windows, with a dirty rag and who knows what in their spray bottle.

The American flag flew big and loud over everything – even the funeral parlour – as if the people were telling themselves over and over who they were and where they were.

The liquor stores and taverns and churches and cleaners were still there, side-by-side, Saturday night and Sunday morning in that usually easy alliance that occurs in black communities, but there was something in the air, in the people, something I had never seen before, a kind of fed-up-to-the-eye teeth-despair.

Folks were tired and fired-up at the same time.

Downtown, Obama's image was everywhere, there were even life-size cut-outs of him in one shop.

Everybody I saw had an Obama something on their person. They wanted, needed him to win.

People gave small donations often, they canvassed, they made sure that everyone was prepared to go out and vote in November.

The 'blues people', as I always consider black Chicagoans to be, had gone inside themselves to make the last big effort.

I'm not talking about the young who were out there in droves and organized, but sceptics like me who just couldn't ever-see-it-happening so-spare-yourself-the-heartache-and-don't-get-too-involved.

'08 had a doomsday feeling to me, but there was something quite simply dogged about it, too.

It was like it must have been when people made the decision to leave their rural roots and come North, no matter what happened.

It was as if folks had gone back to that, back to some ancestral urge. They were going to get on that train once more and ride to freedom.

You couldn't doubt or hesitate about Barack that summer of '08.

I couldn't bring my British scepticism to the table. There was no place for it.

I knew that people had made a shift.

Obama had told them to deal with today and not yesterday, that he could fix today and maybe tomorrow.

But the blues is very much about yesterday, sifting through it, analyzing it.

That is usually what the old time blues guys did.

Blues Queens, well, they were different.

Ma Rainey used to say – as she put on her rhinestone gown sand ostrich feather head dresses – that the folks wanted her to dress up, put her diamonds on, do her hair, if they had wanted to see someone poor and raggedy they would have stayed home and looked in the mirror.

The Blues Queens were about now and living now to the hilt, facing trouble but knowing in your heart that you could over-come it.

"Yes We Can!" was what Ma Rainey, and the late Koko Taylor – Queen of the Chicago Blues – and Bessie Smith sang every day of their lives.

That slogan was always in the very air over the South Side if you just stood and listened.

Barack Obama just came along and plucked it down.

Snob Appeal

Halsted Street is a long, north-south artery. As it enters the South Side it enters 'Bridgeport', traditionally Irish and Italian working class. It is where five mayors have come from, including our current one, and also the home of the infamous 'Regans Colts', a gang that was prominent in the riot of 1919.

Continuing south, Halsted snakes along the borders of Canaryville which housed the mighty Union Stockyards, the meat center of the US. The Stockyards became the battleground for working class blacks and whites after World War One. Then the artery flows alongside Englewood, one of the manin black communities in the city. It is one street away from my home on Ruby Avenue and was the racial barrier when we first moved there in 1960. No blacks crossed it without fear.

It continues south to Chicago's limits at the Little calumet River, into a town called Chicago Heights, where it ends.

North and South, it is the main road that all of the ethnic communities in Chicago have in common.

In Chicago, I grew up near it on the South Side and attended university near it on the North Side. It is a big part of my life.

I had not wanted us to move to the South Side from the West Side.

The South Side sounded snooty.

Just as I suspected, our new life on the South Side was full of snobbery.

There was a club on the corner of Halsted, 'a nightclub' – said in disdain – where the blues was played, mainly to men who were known as 'Players'.

The 'Players' were very Elegba-saturated men: those skinny, shiny bright suits, even in the hot, humid summer; those skinny brims; the canes; the attitude.

When I went to the shop next door to pick up my mother's daily fags, I could hear the music coming from behind the barred window.

The players were very naughty and would begin to assess the local female talent at a rather early age, although they never laid a hand on anyone.

They just complimented you on your progress in the realm of womanhood, in many cases accurately predicting how things were going to turn out.

It was embarrassing, but it was also something deep and wild from a people who lived in a part of town that I didn't understand.

I had heard that some of the players had come from way down South – from the notorious Altgeld Gardens area. Putting people way out there, my Daddy used to say, was a convenient way to get black folks killed.

Polish and Irish working class lived out there, too, the only thing separating them from the bottom of the heap was the colour of their skin, and they fought to maintain that ascendancy.

You had to be hard as nails to live there, and hard as nails to grow up out there.

In our neighbourhood, all of the fathers were blue-collar workers, i.e. working class, i.e. they worked on assembly lines.

These men literally wore sky blue cotton shirts to work, hence the name.

Mom and I dutifully ironed Daddy's shirt every day and prepared his lunch pail with his beloved pork chop sandwiches, which he liked fried and nicely spiced.

His assembly line was in the suburb of Cicero, Al Capone's old headquarters and not exactly a place where black people were greeted with open arms either.

Nevertheless, Dad kept up standards, and being a dapper guy (he even supervised the outfit he was buried in, making sure that the cuffs were just so, etc.) his shirt had to be without wrinkles and the lunch pail shiny. I could never appreciate what he must have had to face every night on that shift, but at least he didn't work near Altgeld Gardens.

At our school we had pupils from there and we knew who they were.

They were the ones who came to school dressed – to our prejudiced little eyes – in dingy blouses with dirt on the collar and the boys had holes in their trousers. Altgeld Gardens kids in those days always seemed to be hungry and the area around their mouths not quite clean. They didn't smell good either, as far as we were concerned, and their mothers would show up after school with their hair uncombed, dressed in flat shoes from which toes whose nails seldom collided with a nail clipper could be seen.

I know that this is a false memory but this is what my new life on Ruby Avenue had turned me into.

Ruby Avenue was determined to keep people from the Gardens out.

We humans always have to look down on somebody.

Even if we have to make it up.

I imagined that the Players came down to the lounge near us to escape the hard bleakness of the Gardens.

There were nothing but smoke-stacks out there for as far as the eye could see, and the air was always foul. Altgeld Gardens was almost near the dreaded Gary, Indiana where the real 'riff-raff' lived, a big steel town that took no prisoners and showed no mercy.

The Jackson Family of Gary, Indiana were kind of our local Von Trapp Family, all-singing, all-dancing, always onstage.

Everybody knew the Jacksons and they played everywhere, but no one thought much of them socially because they were from Gary – way beyond the Gardens itself; living in a tiny house in a city no more than an excuse to keep a bunch of steel mills going.

Of course, because of all of the snobbery and nonsense and just plain lies, I had to have a friend from the Gardens, a wild, rebellious girl whose uniform shirt was not white but a dull grey, and anyway, it was never tucked into her waistband. It hung out and she smoked, too, right near the school.

One day she, my sister and I were invited to sing the *Hallelujuah Chorus* at the local Baptist church.

I don't know how this happened. All of us had been baptized Catholic at my insistence, because there was no way I was going to miss my First Holy Communion with all the bells and the smells and the music and my little white dress complete with veil and the procession (I loved the theatre even then).

I suspect that our dad kept his hand in with the local Baptist church.

Being little girls, we were given the soprano parts and told in no uncertain terms, by an imperious and very camp choir master that we WOULD get it right on the night.

My friend from the Gardens couldn't stop giggling at the man. She just couldn't. Since I was an obedient little thing (on the surface), I tried to keep her quiet, but the man was absurd.

Finally we couldn't help it and both fell over our music books which set the entire soprano section off followed by everyone else.

The church rang with laughter and, I swear, steam was coming out of the man's ears.

The girl from the Gardens had caused this infraction and the girl from the Gardens was duly punished by expulsion.

Some Sundays, during our weekly drive in the Pontiac, we drove out to the Gardens.

There were no trees; huge signs on the edge of the highway advertised places to eat, hair products. Things seemed to be dusty and people walked around looking like those photos from the South that you could see in *Life* magazine. They seemed hot to me and distracted and the whole thing felt like some kind of trap, which it was.

Life was grim and cold-blooded in the Gardens and you trod there carefully if you were not from there.

People checked us out as we waited at the lights. It was obvious that we were not from there.

So the Players from the gardens came down to hang out at the lounge on the corner and hear our blues, which back in the '60's had not become as bourgeois and self-regarding as we had.

Obama has stated that the African American experience is more difficult than the experience of a West Indian immigrant in the US or even his own father's.

When I was growing up, Africans were considered better, more acceptable, even in the segregated south – we'd heard – than African Americans.

When I lived in New York in the '80's, it was the vogue to have West Indian nannies and housekeepers and p.a.'s and meeters-and-greeters because it was assumed that they were somehow 'British' and therefore superior.

The worst part of it was that some of them believed it, too.

A Chicago girlfriend of mine came storming back to our shared apartment one early evening after an afternoon spent in Brooklyn, where she had overhead her date's mother whispering to him when she thought she was out of earshot: "Why you want to bring home this Yankee gal?"

We'd never heard the word 'Yankee' applied to us before!

Moving abroad, moving out of your comfort zone, the place you grew up in, the place that gives you succour, is a kind of act of self-recreation. Just as it was for Obama.

So many black people had decided that Chicago was where they would recreate themselves, find the purpose of their lives.

Chicago, haven of re-creation.

After the Great War, blacks and Irish clashed as they fought for the same jobs, the same living space. The 'Red Summer of 1919' was a summer of race riots so horrific that they are legendary. That summer was the subject of my first adult play.

There was a 'coon song' sung not far away from us in the Irish neighbourhood of the stockyards and it went like this: 'God made the black man/He made him at night/ He made him in a hurry/ And He didn't make him right.'

The Irish ran the town and had a St. Patrick's Day parade that challenged the Kremlin's march-past, to my mind, and I did not warm to the Irish until I moved to London and had a boyfriend with Irish ancestry, who sang my blues-tinged version of *Carrickfergus* in a club in 'County' Kilburn to great warmth. A man said to me afterwards: "You know, I didn't know I was black, too, until I opened my mouth in London."

He called himself a labourer.

I understood that.

The story of *Raisin In The Sun* is the story of the South Side and it conveys it as well as any great blues can.

The African 500

In *Obama: From Promise To Power,* David Mendel recounts how Obama, in his late twenties, gradually begins to make up his mind to have a more stable life.

His restless spirit will have to make way for this. There is always in him the need for speed, the need to keep moving.

Obama, at this time, makes frequent visits back to Chicago, to visit friends, to drive through the neighbourhoods of the South Side that he had worked in as a community organiser before deciding to go to Harvard Law School.

He drives, playing the radio, joining the expressway when he chooses.

For the buzz.

Growing up on the South Side is about highways.

In the President's neighbourhood, where his Chicago home is located, there is South Shore Drive, a lovely expressway that curves along the lake front, all the way to the mid-South Side and then carries on into the northern suburbs on the other end.

In the middle of it is the Downtown area with its magnificent skyline and approaching it from either end at night, is to head into a universe of sparkling lights and buildings – skyscrapers – of extraordinary daring and beauty and grace.

South Shore Drive also rings a series of motor hotels where many of us went on Friday nights in highschool and university, our Michigan Avenue I guess, where you got a room with your boyfriend and drew the curtain for a few hours, a copy of the programme at the local movie house on the table in case you had to lie back home about where you'd been.

Further west and south of the President's home are the 'I (Interstate) 57' and its branch – the Dan Ryan Expressway, known locally as the 'African 500'.

This is a take-off of the fabled stock car race, the Indianapolis 500. Because once you go onto what is also called the 'Damn Ryan', there seems to be no speed limit at all.

The Dan Ryan ran not far from the secondary school that our parents sent me to when Dad could no longer pay the fees at the upmarket Catholic girls' school I had attended right out of primary school. (One of my brothers once told me that the ultimate initiation for guys in their first year at my new school was to run screaming at the top of their lungs, and obviously as fast as they could, across this high speed four lane 'Damn Ryan'!)

Taxi drivers from the airport or the Loop usually didn't like going on the Ryan because that meant going to the South Side, to become immersed in whatever terrors awaited them in THE GHETTO.

That was then.

Actually, the 'Damn Ryan' is still scary.

Interstate Highway 57 is near us, two streets away.

A map will show you that it extends from the state of Missouri to Chicago.

It is also a route from Memphis and New Orleans.

You can even see a sign directing you to Memphis on it.

The Highway ends somewhere on the Ohio River.

This is the river that was once one of the main thoroughfares of the 'underground railroad' – that series of safe houses, churches, and woodland hide-outs through which those who had escaped from slavery could make their way to Canada and to freedom.

Moving.

What you can't really appreciate until you live abroad, until you are far away, living in another culture is this: that Americans will jump into their cars and drive anywhere.

My little brother, when he was stationed in Belgium, thought nothing of driving with his wife all the way to Tuscany.

Hell, he would remind me, folks in Chicago go that far for a party!

When I lived on Ruby Avenue, I would sometimes watch the cars driving down Halsted on to I-57.

I didn't know where they were going but the fact that they were going somewhere, moving, that was important to me.

Out South, where we lived, we had to be careful.

White youths looking for trouble and mayhem would drive up our street, throwing rocks at the precious large windows of the houses in which stood elaborate lamps as showcases of the owners' wealth and taste.

On the corner, at our entrance to the Interstate, was the last place I saw our neighbours from across the street – a boy the same age as my sister and me, a girl the same age as my younger sister, and a boy in between.

I had waved them goodbye as they headed south to see their beloved grandmother.

It was the mid-'60's and Civil Rights workers were being killed and their burned out cars left in ditches. We kids all knew that.

But at the same time it was far away. Distant. Remote.

I was not prepared for the news that came our way a few days later: the local Klan had chased our three friends off the Interstate and over an embankment off the side of a country road where the car burst into flames.

They were on their way back to Chicago.

Nobody was charged.

I can still see their darkened house – all the windows and the doors shut, the curtains down.

And the utter, utter silence.

Their mother took to drink and cursing the sky.

One day they came and took her away.

But the good old I-57 kept and keeps rolling along. That need and that passion for travel, for going further, is still very much a part of life there.

Mobility is what freedom is for black people.

Somebody coming from Hawaii, thousands of miles away, well, that is a big journey.

But very much part of what we South Siders understand.

Regular

It is the beginning of the year 2000 and it is clear that Barack Obama is going to lose the Democratic primary race for a seat in Congress, and that big move to Washington, another step on the ladder to his ultimate goal.

Obama is a senator in the Illinois General Assembly.

Not everyone likes him.

While he is hard-working, he is impatient.

He is impatient with the way things are done in the state capital, Springfield, the base of one of his inspirations – Abraham Lincoln – a hundred years ago.

Obama is impatient to be a part of a bigger arena, faster action.

His poker set – skilled politicians and movers and shakers – advise him not to make the run. The sitting Congressman is the charismatic Bobby Rush, former leader of the Chicago Black Panther Party, from which he moved on to become an official in the administration of the first black mayor of Chicago, the sorely missed Harold Washington. Rush is the member for the Illinois First Congressional District, located on the South Side. It is a 'minority-majority' district, i.e. where the white population is under 50%, like the city of Leicester is here in Britain. The First Congressional District has the highest percentage of black people of any district in the nation.

Rush is a 'homeboy' down to his fingertips and will be hard, if not impossible to beat.

But Obama is convinced that if people will hear him out, hear his plan for bringing the races together, for making politics-for-all work, then they will elect him.

He stresses his Harvard background, his community organising work, his strong links with the powerful people who can do a great deal for the community.

But the connection is not there.

Many in the community see him as a rather brash upstart, moving way too fast, a not yet sure thing too close to the 'baddies' in Hyde Park and the University of Chicago, where he teaches constitutional law.

The University is, as far as many are concerned, an encroacher on land, a destroyer of community cohesion in its attempts to expand.

Plus Obama's clothing is too 'preppy' – a bit like a Sloane/Oxbridge mix.

And worst of all, he looks as if he does not enjoy his food.

There are other things: he's from Hawaii – where he goes every Christmas while his constituents are back home on the South Side literally killing one another over shovelled parking spaces in the stone-hard snow; he had missed a gun control vote downstate while in Hawaii, choosing to stay with a sick Malia and his South Side-born wife who, rumour has it, is heavily suggesting that it might be time for the brother to step up to the plate, go out and earn some real money.

Everybody knows that a grown man with a baby cannot exist on maxed-out credit cards and worn-through socks.

His state assembly constituents know that he can talk about the Bill of Rights until the cows come home, but has he ever just hung out in a club on Friday night, listening to some electric Delta 'blues-shouting' from an open mic?

The complaint boils down to this: Barack Obama is a nice guy, but he's not 'regular.'

Bobby Rush holds the distinction of being the only politician ever to defeat Barack Obama.

'Whupped him' as we say on the South Side

Obama was not seen as 'regular.'

Back in the day, the highest accolade anybody could give you on the South Side was to refer to you as 'regular'.

This was an essential characteristic.

'Regular' roughly translates into not having a 'side'.

But even this doesn't quite get to the meaning of it.

Because 'regular ' describes an ephemeral quality, something that has to do with the way you stand, talk, walk, shake hands, listen, smile, hold your peace, speak out.

It's also about where you situate yourself in the world, who you associate with, what your allegiances are.

Being raised on the South Side in the traditional manner – high-school and a state school if you're lucky – had taught me that you could not be black and be 'regular' at – for god's sake! – Harvard Law, or Oxbridge or any of their equivalents.

Those places existed solely to take 'regular' out of you. Grind it down. Evaporate it.

My working class prejudice again.

Believe me, my very West-London-suburban-public-school husband, would be considered, simply on the face of it, not to be 'regular'

I was quaking in my boots when I took him home to meet my parents.

I knew that there wasn't going to be any problem with Mom, but Daddy might be another story altogether.

His life had been like that of all the other fathers who lived on Ruby Avenue. Hard and full of big and little indignities.

Sure, he would be his gracious, welcoming self, but, well, white folks were not exactly his faves, so bringing a white man home to his house as my husband was not something in his play-book.

So I thought.

As with most things I make assumptions about, I was wrong.

The day after David came back to Ruby Avenue with me, he went to do some shopping with our dad.

He was simply pushing the trolley behind Daddy while Daddy was selecting stuff from the shelves.

That one image stopped what seemed like the entire South Side.

People in the supermarket stopped dead in their tracks for one reason and one reason only: they had seen a white man assisting a black man.

In America. Seriously.

Dad was pleased about the whole thing, not because of the attention, but because, in shopping with him, David turned out to be what he had suspected: 'regular.'

After that, they came home, and went out to the backyard and had a drink amidst my father s vegetable patch.

Dad's vegetable patch was a tiny piece of Mississippi, a slice of the country and rural life, that he could keep close to him.

His own youthful drive to be free, the Army, urban life, all of that, had conspired to take the country away from him.

Like most of the men and some of the women on Ruby Avenue,

he was 'country' through and through. He didn't trust the big city, although he functioned superbly in it. City people lied. But you can't fool a country boy.

To get the vote of people with country roots, people who sing the blues as they are weeding and hoeing their little patches, behind the houses they struggle every day to keep, is hard-won and a great accolade.

Obama had misread the South Side, had not understood his own constituents, people like my father. South Siders like credentials, but that is not what counts. If you aim to come before South Siders, you have to tell them plainly and simply what you're going to do for them.

That's so that they can see the quality of your heart.

They are blues people.

They are 'regular'.

Obama learned the lesson of his failed Congressional campaign.

He learned, after his Congressional defeat, to walk behind the people, pushing that trolley for them. Not for him.

He slowed down after he lost that contest. He put his head down and went back to Springfield.

He taught himself to be 'regular.'

Cat-Eye

'Smitty's'.

South Side.

Obama, the new community organiser, walks into the local barbershop.

The talk dies down.

He's a stranger.

And where did he come from with hair like that?

Nobody wears their hair that high unless they just got out of prison; are on the run from something; sleeping rough; or they're just too close to those hippies nearby at the University of Chicago.

But Obama has to come into this barbershop.

The barbershop is one of the epicenters of the black community.

The people around him might be poor, but they are perfectly coiffed. They will not appreciate his – to them anyway – scruffy, student exterior.

Only white boys from anti-poverty outfits look like that.

Obama knows this.

For him it's time for a change.

As far as his hair is concerned, it's time to get 'clean.'

'Smitty's' has a great reputation.

They can make him 'clean', give him a haircut he can believe in.

Whatever you do, no matter what happens, on the South Side, you have to be 'clean'. 'Clean' is a pristine elegance, a precision in sartorial presentation which always extends to the hair itself. This can be achieved without a great deal of money because being 'clean' is always about a high degree of self-awareness in relation to the public self. How you existed in private – you could live in squalor in a bed-sit with only an electric plate and one pan to cook in – did not matter. What mattered was the moment you stepped into full view, the second that you became part of the public space. At that moment, everything had to be pulled together, shown in its best light.

What the Italians call *bella figura*.

This *bella figura* is achieved with 'legeration' – a word that I've just made up, based on the French word for lightness, lightness of touch, throw-away-chic, off-handedness, understatement, in other words 'cool'.

In other words, a black man's hair had to be cool, and everyone knew what that was.

Otherwise you could be mistaken for a hick; a rube; a rude mechanical.

Or horror of horrors a 'bama' – short for the state of Alabama from where all rubes were perceived to emanate and where they returned to die.

How ridiculous is that? Amongst many others who contradict this notion, Condeleeza Rice is from Alabama. It can be generally acknowledged that she certainly isn't a rube!

My aunt's cleaners was also a focal point of 'clean', located a few miles south of us on South Halsted, right near the elevated tracks, known in Chicago as the 'L'. She and my uncle had started it after he had learned the clothes cleaning trade under the GI Bill after the War. I suppose that he figured that there were three things in those days that you couldn't lose money on: opening a liquor store; a church; or a dry cleaners.

The three had a synergy: the dry cleaners was about Friday afternoon; the liquor store was about Saturday night; and the church was about Sunday morning.

They existed together in an effortless and continuous flow.

South Halsted, down where their shop was, never slept.

This was a bustling neighbourhood, crowded with stores stacked with cut-price hair products, beauty parlours every few feet, small grocery stores, dress stores, shoe shine places.

It was like every community of black people in the big cities of the West: Electric Avenue in London; the Goutte d'Or in Paris.

South Halsted; Electric Avenue; the Goutte d'Or, all three have elevated trains roaring overhead nearby to bring you in. Or take you away.

Movement.

I was constantly told that there were bad men and bad women in those streets where my aunt and uncle did a roaring trade. But no matter. No one walked around those streets anything less than 'pressed'.

'Cat-Eye' had small, piercing eyes and smelled of drink.

His voice was raspy and he didn't seem to have anywhere to go, but he was utterly devoted to my aunt and looked out for her property as best he could.

This was a formidable task.

My aunt and uncle kept cash on the premises, and everyone

knew that.

Anything could happen with cash on the premises, but this was the time before store guards and you just had to watch your back and pray.

'Cat-Eye' knew everyone and he'd point out various dubious characters as I sat at the front desk watching the store, while my aunt and uncle went wherever they went to pick up clothes.

My job was to collect the clothes, write up tickets designating who owned the clothes, what they needed done to them, any special requirements, and the cost.

The smell of some of them took a long time to get out of my nostrils, in visiting a few of the tenements around the shop with my aunt, to pick up the clothes of those who could not bring them in themselves, I had come to recognize that smell as the smell of poverty.

When my uncle brought them back from the factory in his immaculate van, I would cover them in plastic bags, clip the proper ticket on them, and then hang them up in strict numerical order.

I made sure that everything was in its appropriate place.

If you got folks' clothes wrong, or gave the wrong thing to somebody, well, the result could be fatal in that neighbourhood.

I never once saw the police, because they never came around.

I suspect that people preferred it that way.

It was nice and warm there in the winter.

The wind could be howling outside, blizzards driving past the window, but the cleaners was cosy with the bright light from the electrics overhead, and plenty of take-away barbecue ribs, fried chicken and fries, and the blues issuing forth from the radio.

Dinah Washington, singing about revenge and retribution;

other female voices too, who I didn't recognize, and who sounded full of wisdom and stories.

The electric guitars. The pianos. But most of all the guitars, like the human voice in a running commentary on the things of this world.

You had to listen to the guitars and live them, too.

You lived them by holding within yourself a certain sassiness, a kind of playfulness.

The guitars told you that nobody was straight-laced, except the preachers. And they only pretended to be.

The guitars were playful and straight-talking. They travelled with you up from the Delta, and you handed them and their sensibility down to your children and they handed the whole thing down to their children, and no one could appropriate that feeling.

Not really.

It was in the blood.

And that was the truth.

Summer at the cleaners, no matter how many electric fans we had in there, was like an inferno.

Whenever I got a break I would sit in the back, by the open door that led out to the alley and to some sort of cool breeze. Or high up on the fire escape, my head buried in some reading matter.

I would read magazines extolling the lives of upper crust black people who lived their lives in Technicolor, and who always had a smile on their faces. Their houses and cars and hair were glossy. The world around them seemed not to have a care. They wined and dined with the best and I suppose this was all meant to be inspirational to the rest of us, but I never wanted to own a Cadillac, so I didn't care.

Saturday on South Halsted was cheek by jowl in the high road, the smells of cooking food mixed with the blues booming from the record shops.

Guess you can tell that I loved the exuberance.

In my early teens Saturdays were my day to help out, making a little pocket money, and watching with fascination my aunt and 'Cat-Eye' deal with the world.

Good old Cat-Eye was the opposite of my plain-speaking, Mississippi-Delta-born-and-reared aunt, who had helped to take care of me when I was little and who was sometimes mistaken for my mother because we have the same colouring and the same shaped-face.

As I sat at the desk on Saturday afternoons, trying to get used to Cat-Eye's stale alcohol smell and taking in all that my parents had worked their socks off to keep away from us, I could hear Cat-Eye, often deep in his cups, singing along with the songs coming from the record shop across the street.

He had a surprisingly small, tender voice which could make you cry if you did not know it was attached to him. He mostly sang Robert Johnson, completely incomprehensible to me then, but somebody Cat-Eye claimed that he had once encountered in a honky-tonk on the Delta.

The story goes like this:

Cat-Eye was on his way out of town because he had looked a white man in the eye (you averted your eyes when a man came up to you back in Cat-Eye's day. To look a white man in the eye was considered insolent at the very least and a fatal mistake at worst) and had heard that a pack of hounds, accompanying some local good ole boys and their various and sundry firearms, along with a length of rope were being readied for him in the next town.

Now, he wasn't sure if the Robert Johnson he had heard the day before he fled was The Robert Johnson because – as he explained matter-of-factly – in those days people simply appropriated the names of the famous. Everyone did it, and nothing was thought of it. The fun of it was that it confused the white record owners and producers, who crawled all over the region looking for voices; the anthropologists; and all the New Deal types.

He told me that he that he hadn't known if it was The Robert Johnson at all but, thatwhenever he said that he had heard the original great man singing, he was always able to get a free drink and any woman he wanted.

He said these things as casually as if he were talking to someone much older.

I was glad that he couldn't tell that I was blushing.

But he was talking to me the way he would talk to any young woman my age.

Back where Cat-Eye came from a girl my age would have been a mother and fairly well versed in the facts of life.

There were children in the neighbourhood with white mothers.

We would see them walking down the street together, the mothers with closed faces, unhappy.

Some of them were accepted.

Most of them were shunned.

The neighbourhood was the only place these mothers and children could live.

The mothers could not live with black children in their own communities.

Everybody knew that.

These mothers didn't come into the cleaners.

They kept themselves to themselves.

To me, the mothers always looked down-trodden, and thrown-away.

To me, the children looked ignored.

But what did I know?

I was just a kid taking in the gossip of my elders.

I didn't know that they got abuse from both communities – white and black.

All I knew was that the children of these mothers had long, uncombed, untended hair.

"Somebody needs to comb those children's hair", Cat-Eye would say, his voice mixed with disdain and compassion, "Their mamma's don't know what to do with their hair."

It was hard for a white woman who had children by a black man in those days.

Life for them wasn't 'Benneton', it wasn't cute.

Many people in my community looked down on a white woman who would marry a black man. The mothers were sometimes seen as little more than whores.

The children would be perceived as dirty; trash; a dilution of the blood of the black line; vulnerable; and morally dubious.

A wide berth would be made around some of the families because it was even assumed that they smelt.

I don't know how the children of these people saw themselves.

But the children lived and worked and prayed as black people.

It was their mothers who encouraged this, even as they had to stand on the sidelines and watch their own flesh and blood move away from them, even – for some of them – be disowned by the children they had birthed and brought up.

The mothers of these black children had their own blues, which my aunt, Cat-Eye, and me could know nothing about.

Their blues could not, would not, be heard by many on South Halsted Street.

It was one blues that we did not know.

Hyde Park Loop-de-Loop

Chicago 2002

In *Promise*, Mendel lays out the circumstances of the beginning of Obama's ascent, and how his great anti-war speech in which he opposed the coming war in Iraq, is one of the greatest risks that this premier risk-taker has ever taken.

Obama dared to take a position against the potential Senatorial heavyweights for the Presidential races of 2004 and 2008: John Kerry, John Edwards and Hillary Clinton.

Mendel states that he could not have reached this point without the help of one key-group: the 'Lakefront Liberals.'

'Lakefront Liberal' is a generic term which usually means those who live in the upmarket to rich neighbourhoods bordering Lake Michigan, or close by, mainly on the South Side, but also on the Near North Side, as well as further north, all the way up to certain suburbs like Evanston where Northwestern University is located.

A 'Lakefront Liberal' practically always refers to a white person.

You can have the wealth and the influence of a LL, but if you're black or Latin, you're usually not considered to be one because, I guess, we do what we do out of necessity, out of the urgency of the circumstances. An LL has no urgent circumstances in the social sense. LL's do what they do out of political conviction; moral imperative; noblesse oblige; or that untranslatable entity the Irish call the 'craik' – the 'buzz'. I have always suspected that this plays a larger part than people like to admit.

The LL is a Democrat; and sometimes what is known as a 'Yellow Dog' – those who always vote Democrat. No matter what.

As a rule, LL's are extremely well-connected and highly educated and sometimes very rich.

'LL's' by and large support the great cultural institutions of Chicago. They also walk the talk by being out front on behalf of all of the liberal causes such as the anti-Iraq War Movement, etc.

They not only give tons of cash to their favourite candidate, but they can also be 'bundlers' – people who collect more big money from other rich people and deliver it to the Cause.

After highschool, when I had moved to the Near North Side near my university and had become avant-garde, my friends and I often visited an LL in her ivy-covered mansion apartment near the Lake, and near the elegant shops of what we called 'Boul' Mich' after the Boulevard St Michel in Paris.

Ours is called Michigan Avenue.

The LL's apartment was located in a Victorian brownstone.

Needless to say, the likes of us weren't seen very often in the vicinity.

The doorman would look us over pretty forensically whenever we trooped in with our avant-garde selves.

Our hostess wore vintage from the Twenties and would hand pieces out to all of the women and drag queens assembled to hear the latest blues singer, usually a woman, who would stand by the big picture window overlooking the lake.

It felt like Paris in the '20's. In there I met the 'radical chic' set, and learned about Senator Gene McCarthy's bid for the Democrat Party for Presidential nomination as an anti-Vietnam War candidate.

Our hostess pinned the 'Clean For Gene' symbol, of our futile Children's Crusade against the entrenched powers of the 'The Machine' – a big-faced sky-blue daisy – on one of the dresses she gave me, which she swore had been worn by Isadora Duncan in her Bugatti, and which she insisted that I walk the streets of Old Town wearing – preferably without a stitch underneath, in order to attract people to the table where a petition would be set up to gather signatures, in order to get the Minnesota Senator on the ballot.

Well, yeah, it made sense to me, although I didn't, in the end, do it.

I mean, I have so many relatives that I could just see one of them coming down the street and seeing me butt-nekkid ......

It all made sense to me, as did her entertainment, those blues songs sung by obscure but effective singers that reminded me of Ruby Avenue without actually having to live in its 1950's conformity.

She also had a house in Hyde Park, a beautiful structure near the university in which she housed her art collection – what I imagined Gertrude Stein's place must have looked like in the '20's.

Hyde Park.

The area that Barack Obama would settle in, and teach in at the university.

For a long time, Hyde Park meant nothing more to me than the name of a rival basketball highschool, whose doo-wop chant on the court: 'Hyde Park, loop-de-loop' was a challenge to us at 'ooh man Harlan' High.

But Hyde Park was also the University.

Impossible for someone like me to ever imagine attending.

I didn't know that I was four years too early for Affirmative Action. Affirmative Action meant that if you had even slightly lower test scores than a white student, but showed enormous promise, you could get in.

Affirmative Action is about re-balancing hundreds of years of black people being prevented – by law and custom – from realizing their potential.

Hundreds of years of the absence of justice in a climate of moral hypocrisy.

Hundreds of years of thwarted and destroyed potential that have deprived the Republic of its full strength.

Affirmative Action created a climate amongst academics and the whole of society in which black kids were scouted high and low. Not only for their potential, but because they also brought public and private money in their wake.

Through it, little bright black kids who would have been overlooked before, were suddenly hot-housed at very early ages in schools for promising students and in some cases heavily mentored through the system.

There had always been bright black kids, it was just that before AA they stayed bright in their own communities, and for the most part, could only attend the great black universities like Howard, in Washington D.C that we had created for ourselves.

About ten years after I did eventually enter university in the '70's, it had become de-rigueur to try and send your child to a university like Harvard or Princeton or Yale because they REALLY wanted you.

Because you could.

Now, a few black students had always attended Harvard and Yale and Princeton, but with AA in full swing, the gates were wide, wide open.

If you had the test scores and the smarts, they were ready for you, eager for you.

But it took our elders and ourselves to demand that this part of the Constitution be upheld, giving us equal rights and equal access as citizens born on the soil of the Republic.

Our big brothers and sisters had marched peacefully, sat in at roadside diners and had food poured over them; walked through phalanxes of hate just to go to the schools of their choice.

It came down to my generation to administer hard learning and rough justice through urban uprisings and teach-ins at school.

Imagine us students disrupting classes taught by professors with strings of academic credentials behind their names and mountains of publications – informing them in very loud voices that they knew nothing about the subject they were teaching.

That was because they didn't and they knew it.

They had left out entire swathes of the human story and we set out to correct it as we saw it.

We locked them in their offices until they got the message.

We, in our youthful self-righteousnes jumped on their desks and took over.

Looking back, some of those profs should have told us where to get off, but too many of them were too busy trying to be us, to do anything but join us in the streets, on the rooftops, in the parks, at the clubs.

In short, we were quite insolent, which was, to tell the truth, also quite beautiful.

The ones who came after us reaped the benefits of our work, kept their heads down, stayed smart, and moved the story on.

The freedom to speak truth to power was what I learned in Hyde Park.

Before we graduated from highschool, one of my best friends, Dave Buckman, had won a place there at the University of Chicago.

Dave was among the last white intake in our high-school.

The area was changing fast.

White people were fleeing further south and had 'left behind' to us their beautiful highschool and grounds.

Dave was skinny and tall, wore glasses and was spotty.

He looked like a Martian amongst the cool black guys in school, but he had two secret weapons: first, he was a great basketball player and was a walking encyclopaedia on the game; and second, he knew everything about any kind of music you cared to discuss. Any kind.

After Dave moved to the U of C, I went to visit him at his dorm on campus a few days after he'd moved in.

That was when I entered the world of white men and boys.

Before that, they had just been friends at school.

At the U of C, they became something else.

They were all very bright and came from worlds I could only imagine.

White men and boys were the excuse I took to cross the boundaries I couldn't cross in my highschool or on Ruby Avenue.

To my mind, white boys did just about anything and everything, and since this was the heyday of the Pill, which was passed out to you like sweeties, well, there was nothing to worry about.

I thought.

Then, Women's Liberation was about two words: 'women' for the boys, and 'liberation' for the boys, too.

We lay down literally and figuratively and it wasn't until the '70's that we started to wake up and stand up.

But in those days, at the end of the decade we were too busy living our lives to notice. All we knew was that we were different from our mothers.

And that was enough.

It was there at the U of C that I discovered a new blues.

One morning, I woke up in one of my boyfriends' dorm room to discover an album cover on his dresser entitled: *Big Brother And The Holding Company Featuring Janis Joplin*.

There, in Robert Crum's ribald 'keep on truckin'' drawings, was a white girl. Belting the blues.

Through Janis I re-discovered Bessie Smith.

I discovered that Janis had even provided a gravestone for Bessie's grave.

I can still see Janis onstage in her blues queen/hippy girl feathers and beads, belting out her Texas 'good girl' take on surviving a Mississippi flood during the Depression.

It was Janis on those lazy U of C afternoons who taught me – a black girl with a blues inheritance – about a woman's blues, the kind that Ethel Waters sang before she got religion. The kind of blues that were so unlike what the famous male singers sang.

A woman's blues was loud and about transgression and the demand for fulfilment in every sphere, but especially the sexual.

This is true blues queen stuff. Which was how I was beginning to feel. Black girls would not be caught dead looking like Janis and trying to sing like Bessie

But I have to say, deep down inside I knew better than that. Deep down inside I knew that the weird, vulnerable white girl from Port Arthur, Texas had given something back to me that I hadn't even known I'd inherited: a kind of worldly honesty and purity.

Janis was that part of me looking at the world as a strange and a big place, and one I would have to explore.

In Hyde Park, there was connection, connections amongst things that might look disparate at first, even impossible to connect.

But if you could have the imagination, you could do it. Connect. Bring stuff together.

Obama taught at the University of Chicago in Hyde Park.

The best part of the South Side for him to fulfil his destiny.

Black And White In Colour

There is a blue haze in the blues.

If you listen to the music in the right way – and only you know what that is – you can see its colour.

To me, it is a kind of deep, purple-tinged Mediterranean blue, the '*l'air bleu*' that the French call the light around the Mediterranean just after sunset, which is also called 'the magic hour' by cinematographers, because it is one of the most beautiful times to shoot.

The light is soft and smudgy and just about everyone looks great in it.

Looks great.

The notion that the blues make you cry is false, but from inside, the blues can bring up old tears, buried tears, repressed tears.

Yes, it can.

The *New York Times* of Wednesday, 21 January, 2009 is a special issue, in a striking black and white.

I don't remember when I last saw a newspaper with no colour at all.

It looks like an artefact, something that has fallen through time.

I buy it at my local newsagent and open it up right away.

It is a commemorative issue dedicated to the election of Barack Obama as the 44th President of the United States.

He is pictured in a large photo striding through a curtained arch, military men saluting him on each side.

The black and white photo makes him look very young, like your cousin in his highschool yearbook photo, the cousin on the East Coast or the West Coast whom you never see, but who has grown up through a series of Christmas and birthday cards.

The truth is that you don't really know who your cousin is.

But you do know him.

He's your blood.

The photo in the New York Times takes me back to the day before.

Obama is striding through the arches in his dark overcoat and leather gloves.

Like a man heading for his ax – his electric guitar – his blues guitar.

Electrification is one of the hallmarks of Chicago blues and separates it from its antecedents in the Delta

The day of the Inauguration, I wanted to be alone. I asked my husband not to be around. I avoided all of the parties I had been invited to.

The election hadn't even sunk in until a couple of days before, when Obama stepped off Air Force One and I saw him come out of the door with the eagle on it, and I burst into tears

Not that I was sentimental about it.

It was just that it reminded me of the many thousands gone, of the dead.

Of my younger self-on the brink of adolescence, listening to the whistle of the railroad train in the distance.

There is a film that will be in release by the time you read this called *The Day After Tomorrow*.

It is said that the director wished out loud – three years before the date of Obama's Inauguration, before he had even declared his candidacy – that he could cast someone like the junior senator from the state of Illinois in the role of President of the United States.

If his election were possible.

The Day After Tomorrow takes place in the future: 2012.

Over a half century ago, the great African American poet and writer, Langston Hughes, published one of his immortal Jesse B. Semple stories entitled *Simple For President*.

Jesse B. Semple was born in the Chicago black paper *The Defender*, which continues to this day to be one of the most important black papers in the country, a crusading paper that gallantly led the anti-lynching movement after World War One, among other things. It was the perfect vehicle for Hughes to say what was on his mind, and on the mind of the average black person, a perfect publication for a black Everyman.

In *Simple For President*, Semple states this: everyone is sure that there will be a black President by the year 2011. Of course there will be, Semple replies, but by 2011, when a black President will definitely be in place, black people will be too advanced in their access and participation in the American Dream to even need one.

In other words, black people will simply be too cool to get excited about something so obvious as a black President

By 2011 we will have moved on.

Semple states that he wants a black President now ! (In the 1950's).

The prescience of art.

I look again at the *New York Times*'s black and white photos of the Inauguration.

This is the foreign edition, the one that *The Times* is selling abroad.

Are we, who live abroad, being given these black and white pictures as a way of saying: 'you're not here, therefore you don't exist'?

Or have we, like *Simple*, moved beyond, to the next moment, the next arc because we see it all like a movie.

Because we are not there.

Hound Dog

In Europe, on his first visit as President, I listened to Obama talking about his grandfather going to a concentration camp. My dad did, too.

Maybe they had gone together.

Maybe they had been there together.

But they wouldn't have spoken to one another.

Same army, different reality

My father had been part of the second wave on D-Day.

The actual day itself had taken place 24 hours before his 20th birthday.

He had written down 'farmer' on his Army forms, and now he was telling me about his hound dog, the one he used for hunting possum, an activity he adored, when he was a little boy.

We are in Normandy for the 50th anniversary of the landings.

And all Daddy can talk about is a hound dog.

About twenty years before, when I was still at university, I had brought home a Beagle puppy.

I'll never forget my father's face when he saw that dog. He just loved it, and the dog loved him too. I think that my mother eventually had him get rid of the dog because – with seven kids – five still at home – she had enough puppies already.

But he had never talked to me about his childhood dog before, nor about hunting possum to eat and the freedom of it all. Better late than never, it was good to get to know him thousands of miles away from the South Side.

Yes, the President's granddad and my dad were both in the 5th Army under the command of General Patton.

But that's where the similarities stopped.

That's where the similarities stopped for all black servicemen and women in those days.

The Army was racially segregated.

The effort it must have taken to enforce that and fight the Japanese and the Germans, too, must have been mind-blowing.

Dad told us that Patton would stomp around urging his soldiers to go after the Russians, declaring that they (the Americans) were fighting the wrong people.

But my dad and his fellow black soldiers were too busy trying to stay alive against the enemy without and the one within.

When it got bad, my dad said, he'd think about hunting with his dog and bring back to his mind the blues he used to hear from the old folks back in Mississippi, where he had been born.

He had never had a chance to see any of Normandy, of course.

He was too busy driving his supply truck, heading for Germany like everyone else, and trying to stay alive.

He said to me that twilight in Honfleur, that it was in Normandy that he had begun dreaming of owning a house and taking advantage of the GI Bill and the other benefits on offer for vets after the war.

Benefits that he knew that black men and women would have

to fight for.

He knew that he would be coming home to another war.

The North Chicago had been hard, too hard at times, and even at this late stage, at a restaurant in Northern France, he told me that he wanted to return to Mississippi. The land, the river, inspite of everything, they were home.

It was probably better than Illinois anyway, at this point in time, because the civil rights marches and desegregation had dragged change down South into being – kicking and screaming.

He told me that at the 'Battle of the Bulge', the last German offensive, he was finally given arms to carry all of the time.

So many white GI's were dead.

Here he had learned how to talk a woman into bed in French.

He would say some of the words at home to us sometimes.

"Venez-vous avec moi?" and *"Mar-say"*, France, where he had embarked for home.

I didn't know what he was saying until later, after I had learned French.

Lots of naughty stuff!

To see him reciting his bits of French to us little kids now makes me laugh.

Quel homme!

Dad and I went to the restaurant.

The woman who owned it was wonderful, making a great fuss over my dad, and he playfully chatted her up, bragging about Mom at the same time.

Wow. I watched the whole thing in admiration.

The lady was glowing.

And Daddy….his ability to both be a 'drageur' – a guy who can chat-up and brag about Mamma at the same time, well, that was quite a feat!

Before we went to bed, Daddy had a whiskey and talked to me about his dog again. He talked about the song *Hound Dog* too, which Elvis had made into a rock song, but that he knew as something slower, something more like a blues song

The day of my father's funeral, after we had buried him, I went into the bedroom that he shared with our mother, and sat on their bed, the bed in which he had died.

There was a small, clear breeze moving through the room.

The space felt open and still.

And me? I felt happy and at peace.

Because, sitting on the edge of that bed, I could see my dad.

I could see him. He had stopped being our father for awhile.

Instead, he was a small boy again.

Running through the Mississippi woods.

Hunting possum with his hound dog.

Everybody Comes From Something

The whole of *Dreams From My Father* is Barack Obama's attempt to assemble himself from the pieces left behind by his dad.

He is like an Osiris, the great Egyptian god who was dismembered and scattered around the world.

In a sense, Obama is his own Isis, the goddess who, in Egyptian myth, went through the world collecting the bits and pieces of Osiris.

Obama makes himself whole again.

He ends *Dreams* a few streets from where I grew up in Ruby Avenue.

He is no longer searching.

He is home.

There is a moment when you're a little kid when you are convinced that you're a foundling, that somebody left you on a doorstep, and that your job is to go find that person.

What you might do with them when you find them, what you might say, or think, or feel, is never part of the equation. It's the search that counts.

All of those great blues queens travelled. They were always on the move.

When the bluesmen travelled – hitching rides on freights – they were called 'hobos', a much more respectable term then than it is now.

You might say that Genet was a hobo, or Brecht. Even in the midst of their grandeur, Paris and Berlin seem to me to have been hospitable to the person who just turns up, without a bed for the night. The hobo.

And this makes Paris and Berlin, to my mind, blues cities.

There is the grey of Paris, that light grey colour which is like melancholy, contemplation, interiority made manifest. And what hasn't Berlin seen in its time?

The Order of nuns who taught at my primary school had been co-founded by a priest who had escaped the 'Terror' during the French Revolution, and had made his way to Baltimore, where he teamed up with a black woman – Mother Elizabeth.

The Oblate Sisters Of Providence are today a mainly African American community – Negro they would have called themselves when I was at primary school who have been teaching black children since before the Civil War.

They were a pretty straightforward bunch who took no prisoners.

There were daily public wackings of boys who didn't know how to obey, bent over chairs – behind to the class – as Sister went at them with a yard stick, dust flying off their corduroy trousers.

One boy got beaten for playing, at top volume, the *Duke Of Earl* in the playground on his transistor. When we heard it during Latin lesson, we all started chanting: 'Duke, Duke, Duke, Duke Of Earl...'

He was whacked.

Another kid was caught singing a pretty ribald blues song in order to impress a girl he liked. We didn't know what the words meant, but Sister Carmela did, so he was sealed up for one hour in the cloakroom.

We knew that we were the deeply loved children of people who had endured segregation in the South, segregation at work, and the hardship of scraping together enough money to buy a home when no downtown bank would lend a black person a penny.

This lack of access to a bank had left them open to the most unscrupulous of their own people. My dad once took one of his guns and went out looking for a black lawyer who had stolen his deposit for a house. This was a weasly little guy who always wore the same brown suit – in all weathers – and carried a briefcase. Dad got his money back – with interest.

In school, Sister Carmela called us "border-line Negroes", not a mental condition, but like black folks born in Maryland on the Mason-Dixon line. Just as, she implied, they might not know whether they were Southerners or Northerners, we simply didn't get that we had an obligation to our parents and to those behind them. There were no excuses and don't blame the white man.

We had to grow up.

For some reason, there was small paintings of Paris and Berlin in Sister Carmela's room.

Maybe now, when I think of it, these paintings, these melancholy watercolours, which looked like imitations of Millet, may have set me on my path to Paris.

There was space to day dream in Sister Carmela's class, during the time when she insisted that we read silently. I would finish quickly and then enter the world inside my head, a world which was far, far away.

And Berlin? Berlin was my love of history.

Berlin was part of my childhood because we were taught 'duck and cover',get under the desk in case of nuclear attack. We lived with the mushroom cloud over our heads and possible obliteration at the drop of a hat.

One of my classmates, Tyrone Blake would say anything, usually what you didn't have the nerve to say, like: "Why don't the priests and the sisters get married?" because, of course, we girls would weave the most romantic fantasies about the handsome young priest and the lovely young nuns. Nothing sexual, just dreamy.

A family next door to the school kept chickens behind a wire fence. During class we could hear the grandfather singing the blues to himself as he fed those chickens and talked to them. Sometimes he would come wandering out onto the street, kind of embarrassing because he wore overalls and the same red-checked jacket day in and day out, no matter what weather it was.

One afternoon when it was really hot and we were trying to practise the dreaded Palmer Method of penmanship, trying to keep our handwriting neat and on the straight lines, Tyrone looked up and, out of the blue, asked whether the old man with the chickens... was he a hobo?

Our nun, Sister Carmela asked him what he meant.

Tyrone explained that he just seemed to come out of nowhere all the time, out of nothing.

He knew that he was somebody's granddaddy, but where did he come from?

Sister Carmela asked him why he mattered to him.

Tyrone replied that he just seemed to be different, from nowhere.

Sister Carmela tapped him hard with her index finger in the

middle of his forehead, a quite precise form of torture.

"Everybody comes from something," she said, "Just because you don't understand that, doesn't mean it's not true. Nobody's unique. Not if you look hard enough!"

Crossing Over

Chicago.
The summer of '09.
I am on the South Side, in Obama's neighbourhood, not far from the family home, the front of it covered by tall trees.

There are a gaggle of police cars out front, the policeman sitting leisurely inside, waiting for their shifts to be over.

Today there are no tourists, no pilgrimages are being conducted.

The few locals on the street this time of day seem bored.

The street has an eerie quiet.

It feels as if it's been dropped down from another place.

I wonder, if I were to go around the back of this street, if I'd find that it was no more then part of some Hollywood film, just wood and slats holding up a series of facades, with a film director sitting in a chair waiting to yell 'Cut!'

"Obama's election ain't done that much for us. Not really. We're proud, we love him, but not much has happened. Tell the truth, I didn't expect that. I voted for the BEST President, not the BLACK President, and that was Barack. You know what? I'll vote for him again, I don't care what he do or don't do. What the Democrats don't get is – we didn't vote for THEM! So they shouldn't be so sure of things. We voted for BARACK. As long as he's a Democrat, we're Democrats. Period. So, I say: 'Don't be so complacent, donkey-folks!"

The donkey is the symbol of the Democrat Party.

Her voice grows quiet.

"You know, let me say this, sometimes I think that with Obama the bar's been raised just too high. Too high. We here, us on the ground, we haven't got the blowback. White folks think: 'I voted for Obama, so I'm off the hook. I can criticize, demonize.' It's always about race here. Don't forget that.

"Barack says look to today, and he's right. But a lot of us, we just can't because the wounds are too deep. You know what gets me? This new, smart generation comin' up, complainin' that people like me hold them back because we're lost in the Civil Rights time. Hell, they don't think that's not still goin' on? How do they think that they got into Harvard and Yale and Wall Street, 'cause they smart? Black folks have always been smart! We just couldn't go to the school of our choice.

"It was people like me who hit the streets back in the day and now these kids are in power but they act like they got amnesia. Black folks never used to forget what the old folks did for them. But I'm happy. I don't like drama. I don't even watch it on tv For what? Enough of that around here.

"Child, don't let me start. I got work to do."

She gets back to work. Then she turns back to me:

"Barack's still regular. Know what? If you see a lot of dead roses in the Rose Garden at the White House that's 'cause Barack is out back smokin'!"

There is an altercation in the street. It sounds like it could get nasty. I freeze inside. Who knows what's about to kick off? I think then about why I'm not part of the craze back in Britain for The Wire. I've lived 'The Wire'. The woman I'm talking to, everybody out there on the street, they really LIVE 'The Wire'. Do they watch it?

The woman's not fazed. She whispers, bringing me back to her, "I knew he was goin' to win"

"How?" I ask.

"His grandmamma passed the day before the election. She went to the other side so she could do her work for him. 'Toot' still lookin' out for him like a grandmamma supposed to do."

Here it is, right before me, that blues aesthetic: death is a bridge.

When I was at university, a visiting black professor, a woman with locks down her back, once made an off-hand remark that "black folks didn't die until they became Christian."

At the time I didn't understand, but I've come to know what she means.

The blues has this quality of the 'other world', of that great African Triad of the living, the dead, and the unborn.

This Trinity exists together and at once in the African consciousness and it was brought over with the Passage.

The blues are full of the knowledge of this.

Growing up, we respected the dead because, well, they weren't gone.

Backwater Blues

Obama states in *Dreams* that when he said that he wanted to be a community organiser a man told him that anyone who wanted to do that had to be maladjusted.

Later, he is offered a job in Chicago by an organiser who tells him that he has been trying to pull together urban blacks and suburban whites in a bid to save manufacturing jobs.

He needs someone to help him do this.

He needs someone black.

The only thing that can save you while you're on the road is your ability to mirror – not to mimic – but to let people know that you understand, that you hear them.

This is the empathy that creates the blues

Obama loads up his old banger with the few belongings he has and drives to Chicago.

There he notices how hard black people work, how clear-sighted they are.

He knows that Chicago is the town that kills the big Broadway show, the town that doesn't believe the hype.

Years later, he comes back to Chicago, comes back home.

It is the night he has won the Presidential election and only

Chicago, being in Chicago, sharing his triumph with Chicago, makes it real.

The late columnist Mike Royko was appalled when certain segments of the town went mad over the late Princess Diana when she visited and danced with local bigwigs.

His was the only column in America that thundered against the royal visit. He asked: hadn't America fought a war against kings and queens?

That's Chicago.

One of the ways that I paid my way through university was to work at a blues club on the Near North Side,

I think it's still there today, I don't know. I don't like going back to places where I had once had a wonderful time.

I don't want them to be changed.

There were three wonderful guys behind the bar who made the drinks, and a man who was there frequently was Bruce Iglauer, founder of the great blues label, Alligator Records.

Bruce booked his artists into the club because the customers were serious music lovers, and everyone knew and appreciated what they heard there.

A big, tall husky woman strode in one night at the last minute, dressed in country overalls, the kind with the bib, and she wore a big workman's shirt, boots and carried a huge rock and roll ax.

When she got on the stage she filled it completely with her personality and her presence, and whatever you were doing you stopped it then and there to see what she would do.

She surveyed the audience quietly and then growled as if she'd been talking to us for about three hours: '...ok, yeah, I know that Elvis recorded *Hound Dog*. But that's my song. And this is how I sing it.'

And she sang it.

Elvis's rendition sounded like a happy-go-lucky ditty compared to Big Mamma's much slower rendition. It sounded like prophecy and a warning, and, to my ears anyway, a more authentic version.

Koko Taylor was at the club often, tenderly looked after by her beloved husband, Pops.

She was small and round and wore a deep black short curly wig. Her body was compact and full of energy. Her chocolate brown face was continuously creased in a wide smile, but her eyes were always checking you out, the way that they say Louis Armstrong did.

'Ace', now Rich, one of the bartenders then and who now owns a string of restaurants in Southern California, told me recently that there was a night that Koko was meant to play and there was no audience.

He said that as he lit the candles and got the tables together, he was worried. But not Pops.

Five minutes before Koko was due to go on the audience flooded in, cool and as relaxed, summoned by some invisible power, arriving just in time and on time.

Koko often performed her signature tune, an answer to Muddy Waters' bravado hymn to machismo: *I'm A Man*.

Koko answered him right back with I'm A Woman, full of the same bravado, menace, sexual innuendo, dread and joy that his was.

When I went home to the South Side for Sunday lunch, I could see in the women of Ruby Avenue everything Koko sang about.

I'd sit in the backyard with some of the older people, listening to them re-tell stories about the South, knowing that my new friends at the University couldn't possibly fit into the world I had grown up in.

The truth is that I wasn't then, and am still not, half the woman my mother and the other ladies of her generation on Ruby Avenue are and were. Or that Koko was.

Something in me knew that then, which is probably why I would shore myself up by re-listening to Dinah Washington's version of *Backwater Blues*. Dinah rebooted me, took me away from all the hippy and folksy and rock and roll madness that being at university in the early seventies on the North Side was about.

I knew this: my life had changed going away to university.

I would never live under my mother's roof again. I have spent most of my life now not under her roof. But the blues I listened to while I lived with her, that I still see in her when I go back to Chicago, remain with me and always will.

Watch The Lights

Paris, the early summer of '09.
The Obamas are in town, after attending the D-Day commemorations in Normandy.

I am not far from Notre Dame. The streets around it are silent, devoid of people and roped off.

People line the streets near the cathedral, waving little flags and carrying adoring signs.

A group of American university students stand in the front of the crowd, nearest the entrance to Notre Dame. One of them is holding a sign which reads: 'Please wave at us. We've been standing here all day waiting for you!'

A friend of mine, who has come from his hometown of Caen in Normandy has been there all day.

There are signs around town that read: 'Yes, oui Caen'.

He says that he loves Obama, but that even he found the signs a bit naff.

I leave him and walk away from the cathedral, toward its back, its famous flying buttresses sprawling like a great dowager settling her skirts.

I imagine how the First Family will find the cathedral, and I recall the day a few weeks earlier, when a Chicago friend and I casually walked in at the beginning of Mass to find it filled at the front with black people and a black priest in the pulpit.

I had never seen this before and decided that it was a lovely omen for Obama's visit.

In one of the streets around the cathedral that has been sealed off, I see in the window of a record shop an old Moms Mabley album.

I have to blink twice to make sure I'm not dreaming.

Yes, its Moms, her cheeky, toothless smile, a cap perched on her head and dressed in her long, old lady's dress.

Moms.

Our parents had to keep Moms' records away from us. She was considered 'adult', like Redd Foxx was, and a few other comics were and therefore put on the equivalent of the top shelf down in the basement.

Moms was born Loretta Mary Aiken in 1894 in Transylvania County, North Carolina, one of twelve children.

She took her stage name Jackie Mabley from an old boyfriend, because, she explained, he had taken so much from her!

For every black Chicagoan of a certain age 'Moms' was simply the Queen of comedy.

Mabley adopted a stage persona based on an old lady, cantankerous, sassy and in-your-face.

She wore a kind of dressing gown onstage and often a floppy hat.

A lot of her routine centred around her 'obsession' with young men.

('Moms' was rumoured to have been a lesbian and is a gay icon. She was a headliner in the '30's at the South Side's famous

Club DeLisa, which was known in the '30's for its gay floor-shows.)

She would prowl the stage stating that she would have nothing to do with an "old man", but God knows how old that might be.

You know who hipped me?

My grandmother.

This is the truth!

She lived to be 118 years old. And you wonder why Moms is hip today? Granny hipped me.

They lied to the rest of them, but I'm not gonna let you be dumb!

One day she's sitting out on the porch and I said, "Granny, how old does a woman get before she don't want no more boyfriends?" She was around 106 then.

She said, "I don't know honey, you'll have to ask somebody older than me!"

This humour was part of my childhood. I didn't understand it, of course, but I loved Moms' personas. She'd sing her blues songs, stop, talk. She was so down-to-earth.

I suspect that Whoopie Goldberg owes more than a little bit to Moms!

Chicago's Chess Records was considered quite simply the greatest blues label in the world.

Little Walter, Memphis Slim, John Lee Hooker, Bo Diddley, Howlin' Wolf, all were on their label at one time.

Legend has it that The Rolling Stones, at the beginning of their career, came walking, meekly and in awe, into Chess' South Side headquarters to pay homage.

They found Muddy Waters painting the ceiling!

Moms wound up at the Playboy Mansion on the Near North Side, where the edgiest and hippest black performers worked.

Chess re-issued her performance there under the title: *Moms Wows*.

We kids would sit at the top of the basement steps unseen and unheard, entering Moms world, a world that our parents had refused to leave behind when they attained suburban respectability.

My parents and all of the adults on Ruby Avenue loved Red Foxx too.

His records were worse than Moms, and only came out late into the garden parties when our parents were too tired to dance and sat in lawn chairs drinking and laughing and reminiscing. Red Foxx was a superstar.

He was born in Missouri but raised on the South Side.

He starred in the '70's American version of *Steptoe And Son*, a comedy about two black junkyard owners in LA.

But *Sandford And Son* simply solidified Red's fame. He was so famous that it was said that he was the only person outside of Elvis's immediate circle to be invited to his wedding!

He had worked with Malcolm X in the '40's when Malcolm X was known as Malcolm Little. In his autobiography, Malcolm calls him 'Chicago Red' because of his red hair, a lighter shade than Malcolm's own.

Red Foxx dropped dead on the set of his sitcom, *The Royal Family,* and people thought it was part of one of his routines.

Jamie Foxx named himself after Red, and Chris Rock cites him as an influence.

Moms and Red were counter-balanced in our childhoods by *The Mickey Mouse Club* – the original one.

Needless to say that there were no kids on it like us. The only time we saw young faces like ours they were getting high-powered water hoses aimed at them during sit-ins.

But we didn't expect to see ourselves on tv. We were masters of self-projection and we joined in like good kids, being a happy part of the milk and cookie Americana sold to us.

One of the Moms' jokes I used to recite over and over when I was a little kid (and in her old lady, toothless voice, too) was this one: "Folks talk about the good old days. What good old days? I was there, where was they at?" And there is a motto of hers that I live by today: "You know, everybody tells little kids before they cross the street: 'Baby, now watch the lights. Watch the lights!' Damn the lights! Watch the cars! The lights ain't never killed nobody!"

Or perhaps they have.

Kill the honeymoon, the dreamy illusion.

What I mean is this, that as more and more light is shed on the Obama Presidency, it will reveal a subtle light of its own, a light that emanates from the blues, a blues that will be simple and stark and will stick to its principles.

This Obama Music will sing what it is and live it, the way Big Mamma Thornton did, and Koko Taylor.

It won't matter if this blues exists for one term, because in every moment of it, it will be 'regular'; no-frills; and straight from the people.

Alone

Chicago. 2004.
Obama sits at his desk in his home in Hyde Park.

It is late night and he is in his tiny room, with the desk where he writes his speeches, and reads and thinks.

In *Promises*, we read that this room is called 'The Hole' by his wife.

Obama was brought up as an only child.

Everyone knows that he treasures his space, his time with himself.

He is composing his soon to be famous keynote speech for the convention at which the Democrats will nominate John Kerry for President.

Four years earlier, another handsome, charismatic young black politician had spoken at the convention, but his speech had been flat.

Obama is running for the Senate.

He can't be flat.

Out of 'The Hole' will emerge the 'Red State. Blue State' speech, the speech in which he will say that there are no colour codes, only Americans.

In a few hours the world will hear this speech.

But first he has to compose it in 'The Hole'.
Alone.

Even surrounded by others, there is something that is solitary about Barack Obama.

This may be an odd thing to say about a man who is probably never alone. But you can imagine, can't you, this man looking for a solitary space, quiet time for himself.

Just as all of the blues greats seem to be alone, playing all alone, whether surrounded by others or not.

Obama is a bluesman precisely because of this quality of alone-ness.

This is different from aloofness in that this blues isolation, this inner quiet has to do with listening, listening for the 'blue note', a jazz chord whose essence is rooted in the blues.

We all live in a world which day by day is becoming more clamorous, that is stripping away our privacy.

But I believe that we are listening, trying to hear that blue note, trying to hear our own blues.

GOSPEL

In The Upper Room

Take My Hand

In *The Audacity Of Hope* Barack Obama writes of how he was drawn to the black American church because of its power and its commitment to spur social change.

He finds that the black church deals with the whole person, the person-in-the-world.

It serves as the centre of the black community's social, political and economic life. It eagerly embraces Christ's call to feed the hungry and clothe the naked.

Obama writes the type of black sermon that freely acknowledged that church-goers can leave church still feeling the same old lusts, the same old fears, and hatred.

But he finds that it is in gospel music that black people find a kind of release, a salvation.

He had found it there too.

If you don't know gospel music; if you don't like gospel music; if you dismiss gospel music as something minor, primitive, strictly for Sundays only, then you will have missed 80% of Obama's campaign and arguably a good deal of his Presidency.

His mother steeped him in gospel and for good reason: it is the base, the root, the juice, the very definition of it all.

The intonation and rhythm of his voice, that inclination of his head for emphasis (the way in which he slightly lowers it and speaks hard into the microphone); the jutting of his finger at key points, all of this is pure Grade A 100% gospel.

Forget about all of the intricate analysis involving 'nudge' marketing, etc.

That kind of stuff was only the veneer, the cross-over.

I'm talking about inner signals from what is called America's most segregated hour-church on Sunday mornings.

When the black community – which had been skeptical about this young man with the funny name, out of Hawaii of all places, and born of a white mother – saw him take to the stage that cold Iowa night in the early days of his campaign and make a slight tilting gesture with his head, they knew that he was alright.

That he was from the church.

It is from the black church – South Side of Chicago division – that Barack Obama truly set forth.

He will return there in the fullness of time, as if he had never been away.

There is something intrinsic in the phenomenon of Obama himself, and the places he has come from and has taken us to that has to do with gospel.

In New York in the '80's, there was a vogue for a moment concerning the great African American divas: Shirley Verret, Grace Bumbry, Jessye Norman; Kathleen Battle, and the vogue was about the glory of their voices. You could hear the church in their 'Carmens', their 'Mimis'.

There was such a fascination then with the 'natural' musicality of the 'black female voice' that even the New York Times Magazine did a story on it.

I was studying classical voice at the time and my teacher was thrilled because he had one of these incredible creatures (i.e me, by dint of my ethnicity, I had to be good and potentially great) in his classroom.

True, I had come from some of the same places that great sopranos and mezzos and contraltos had, but I wanted to sing Broadway show tunes.

Yet the 'aura' still clung to me anyway

My teacher's other students would smile at me in awe when I came in for my lesson. I was a diva-in-the-making, right?

And what made this so? Was it our physiognomy, our life experiences?

Opera singers and teachers were especially interested in Aretha Franklin, a musical descendant of the 'Queen Of Gospel', Chicago's Mahlia Jackson. The way that Dr. King had delivered his speeches was also being studied.

Made sense to me.

I could 'see' Aretha's technique. It made pictures. And I could hear the symphony that was the King voice. So 1 knew what all the fuss was about in the conservatories and concert halls. I knew about the music.

Moving to London soon after, I accepted that I didn't have the discipline nor the technique to pursue a career, I cut the US loose for five years – I didn't want to be homesick.

But I didn't cut gospel loose.

'Gos-pel' as they say in France, elongating the 'o', stretching the last syllable to breaking point, as if it is climbing that hill to Calvary.

They're obsessed with gospel, particularly one song: *Oh Happy Days*, which I think has become their alternative national anthem!

It was in Paris that I first heard the voice of the magnificent Liz McComb, a Cleveland Ohio maestra who grew up listening to Mahlia.

Her music has led me to La Velle-born Lavelle Mckinnie Duggan, she's from Kankakee, a southern suburb of Chicago, so she's an honorary South Sider, as far as I'm concerned.

Both of them heiresses of a great tradition, carrying it forth around the world.

Two creators of that tradition immediately come to mind.

Lance Latham Benton, was a prominent evangelist and preacher, and renowned pianist for the Chicago Gospel tabernacle. He was of concert calibre, and an arranger of music, and authored books on theology and his own Christian movement. He did an enormous amount in the creation and laying down on paper of gospel.

And Robert Bradley, one of Martin Luther King's favourite singers, a man who had lived for some time in London, who was knighted. He became director of music for the National Baptist Convention and was recorded as part of 'Chicago Gospel Legends'.

But it is Thomas Andrew Dorsey, called the father of gospel music, who helped make gospel music what we know today.

He would say things like: "I had hope, faith, courage, aspiration, and most of all determination to accomplish something in my life...and I've been thrown out of some of the best churches in America."

This indicated his difficult start in his attempts to take church music to another level.

Dorsey was the son of a Baptist preacher; his mother was the church organist.

At one time they both had to do manual labour in order to hold the family together.

In those early years, Dorsey faced two paths: the religious and the secular.

He left his native Atlanta for Chicago as soon as he could and became a jazz pianist.

He performed with Ma Rainey where his style was called 'whispering'. He was a great draw at after-hour parties during Prohibition because he could play so quietly that the police never knew that illegal drinking was going on.

He had a nervous breakdown as a result of his busy schedule, married his love of long-standing, went back to work and had another breakdown.

After that he began composing sacred music, attempting to move the acapella tradition – exemplified by the Fisk Jubilee Singers – into a more complex musical realm, a realm where the blues dwelled.

His sacred music used syncopated notes in an eight-bar blues structure; but, instead of blues themes, his songs told stories of hope and affirmation. Dorsey described it as 'good news on either side'.

His first gospel song, *If You See My Saviour Tell Him That You Saw Me*, was published in 1932.

But he was rejected by churches left and right.

After he lost his beloved wife in childbirth, he wrote one of the most famous gospel songs of all time, *Take My Hand, Precious Lord*, a song which he would always say came directly from God.

This song has been recorded by everybody from Aretha to Elvis. Martin Luther King loved this hymn above all and had it sung at the rally the night before his assassination. He had always asked that it be sung at his funeral. And it was.

Unhappy with the way gospel artists were being treated, and after the success of *Precious Lord,* Dorsey used his experience as an agent to publish the music himself.

Dorsey co-founded the National Convention of Gospel Choirs and Choruses in 1933. Six years later, together with his protégé and exemplar of genius, the immortal Mahalia Jackson, Dorsey ushered in what is still called 'Golden Age of Gospel Music.'

It is to her recordings that the brilliant and prescient anthropologist mother of Barack Obama, Dr. Ann Dunham, wisely turned when she wanted to teach her only son what it means to be a black man in a white world.

Going To Meet The King

January 20, 2009.
The Inauguration of Barack Hussein Obama as the 44th President of the United States.

The featured singer takes to the podium.

Among other things she is: Rolling Stone's #1 all time best singer of the rock era, ahead of Ray Charles at No. 2, Elvis Presley at No. 3, Sam Cooke at No. 4 and John Lennon at No. 5; and the first black woman to appear on the cover of *Time Magazine*.

Aretha Franklin, one of the daughters of the celebrated Detroit minister and renowned preacher, the late Rev. C. L Franklin, pastor of New Bethel Baptist Church, takes the podium, at the base of the red and blue velvet carpeted stairs of the Capitol.

A Gospel piano begins and Ms. Franklin opens her glorious lungs to deliver a full-on 'goin' back to church' version of *My Country 'Tis Of Thee*.

It is especially poignant to me that she does not sing, 'land where our fathers died', but instead: 'land where my father died', in honour of her beloved father, and also to remind the audience that he and those like him have fought nobly for the

United States, and have always been a part of the Republic, long before its inception.

This is gospel, and that is as it should be.

Perhaps only the South Side Of Chicago, could have sent the first black President to the White House. No other city has the history of cohesion and power in concentration that the black South Side has.

The history of its religious institutions, their longevity, stability, drive, culture, and what could be called sheer bloody-mindedness in surviving and thriving, is one of the pillars that has built the colossus that is the area that sent Barack Obama to the Oval Office.

Those ecclesiastical institutions – no matter what faith they adhere to – are 'testifying' institutions: i.e. they 'bear witness' in this world. Right now.

And gospel music is the sound that they live by.

Some might say that I am culturally deprived.

Because I was raised Roman Catholic and deprived of the black church –, of the Bible, and of the gospel in regular doses.

Not that we had Gregorian chant ringing through our house on Ruby Avenue, it's just that we didn't sit through three hour sermons, exquisite gospel choirs, Sunday meals in the basements and on the lawns of the church, none of that belonged to us.

But even though we were all baptized and more or less practicing Catholic, our roots – like all people's roots on the south Side – are dug deep within the Southern Christian church: Baptist, Pentecostal, etc.

Gospel music was the underbelly of our world and, whether

you went to church or not, you knew some of the songs, which could ring through my head even at Mass when I sang a Provencal hymn to Our Lady.

We're the aberration because our family has always been full of ministers, and I suspect always will be, male and female, church and street corner.

And Jesus lives very close and immediate.

One of my aunts, who lives in a retirement home not far from the Obama family home, said to me, the summer of his first year in office: 'Look. Kennedy was a better speaker than Obama. Bill Clinton was a great speaker. They were both better at it than Obama. I know. I was there. But that's got nothin' to do with it. God put Barack where he is. And God's gonna keep him there.'

Laugh if you like, but it's that faith bound up in church, the first and last refuge, that kept and keeps black people going.

This is why Barack Obama came to the black church.

In *Dreams* he writes that church was where the people were.

There is no exact date for the start of Black Gospel, although some musicologists who are experts in Black Culture, etc. will disagree.

Incidentally, this is one of the reasons that orthodox Islam, the Black Muslim religion, and Black Judaism rose to prominence and power in the black community during the height of the Black Power Movement in the '60's because of Christainity's supposed link with subjugation.

Its perceived meekness and turning-the-other-cheek-ethos is the reason that Obama himself has written that his father preferred Islam.

The enslaved did, however hold on to their deities, hidden in Vodun (vodoo) and Santeria, in their dances, and in the music.

The enslaved held on these orisha through the music from the Old Country, putting them into what are now defined as jubilees – joyous songs of praise, sung in church; work songs; and Gospel, which took many forms.

At the end of the 19th Century, early 20th Century, people of African descent had attained, through the 14th and 15th Amendments, citizenship and the right to vote.

These constitutional rights were rolled back during the era of 'Reconstruction', that period after the American Civil War when the South was brought back into the Union. One of the ways this was achieved was to give them back control over state law, which they immediately used to institute what were known collectively as 'Black Codes'. 'Black Codes', euphemistically known as 'Jim Crow', established so-called 'separate but equal' facilities, education, transport, even drinking water fountains.

The 40 acres and a mule 'promised' at Emancipation were rescinded.

Black people were effectively enslaved once again, stuck on the land from which they had been liberated, and forced to work it as 'sharecroppers', tenant farmers who paid their crop in exchange for basic necessities and the roof over their heads.

Out of this atmosphere came the religious movement known as 'revival' – an intense turning to God as the only hope in this world – became popular.

Revival led the 'sanctified' or 'holiness/pentecostal' movement, which allowed worshippers to play any instrument they wanted in church, not just the organ.

So in came tambourines electric guitars, etc.

Sanctified' was happy, rural, based in the countryside, direct, simple, all about you and Jesus with no one in between.

Gospel emerged out of this based around a direct relationship to God, rooted in the self, and not through any permission from a leader or a group. Gospel became testimony about the miracle of conversion and grace in action. Right now.

By the way, r'n'b is rooted here, utilizing the same method and meaning, but diverting it to the secular.

It was this diversion that caused such an uproar, when a great gospel star like Sam Cooke became a r'n'b artist.

It is this gospel root that is at the base of everything Aretha Franklin sings.

It is this root that made Michael Jackson's funeral not a pop event, but a gospel one.

Jennifer Hudson brought her Chicago gospel roots to express everything that the Jackson family wanted and needed to have said about them and their beloved.

This was accomplished, too, by the Los Angeles based Andrae Crouch Singers in their dirge *Going To Meet The King* as Michael's coffin was brought onstage by his brothers. Crouch himself is considered Thomas A. Dorsey's successor as 'King Of Gospel'.

The entire funeral was filled with signs and references that only those who know and love gospel could completely see, understand and be comforted by.

His family, in the end, had taken Michael Jackson not back to Neverland, but all the way back to where they and he had begun: in Midwest Gospel.

Back to church.

The Weaver

Barack Obama dedicates *The Audacity Of Hope* to 'the women who raised me': his paternal mother 'Tutu' and 'my mother whose loving spirit sustains me still'.

Summer '09.
A friend sends me the following press release:
'Textile Museum
Washington, DC, USA
For two weeks only, textiles from the collection of Ann Dunham, President Obama's mother, are on view at The Textile Museum. This marks the final stop on a national tour of the exhibition 'A Lady Found a Culture in its Cloth: Barack Obama's Mother and Indonesian Batiks'. Early in her life, Ann Dunham explored her interest in the textile arts as a weaver, creating wall hangings in earth shades of brown and green for her own enjoyment.

After marrying Lolo Soetoro and moving to Indonesia in the 1960s with her son Barack Obama, Ann Dunham was drawn to the vibrant textile arts of her new home and began to amass the collection from which the exhibition objects are drawn. The wide variation in the batiks reflects the range of colours and of patterns, both classic and contemporary, that captured her imagination, and provides a window into the rich culture from which these fabrics originated.'

I have to be upfront here: I feel great respect and love for the late mother of Barack Obama, Stanley Ann Dunham of Kansas and the world.

She was so unlike me. Coming from Ruby Avenue, South Side of Chicago.

I was brought up to play it safe.

So was she, but she refused.

Stanley Ann was like the graduate women I encountered when I started university in the '70's: clear, righteous, hard-headed, soft-hearted, bright as a shining star, consistent and clear.

She was the kind of woman who would remind her staunch Kansas parents, right in front of her black son at the height of Watergate, that they had voted for Nixon.

Her generation of women were one-offs, but they left behind daughters and little sisters to follow in their footsteps.

I'm proud to be one of those little sisters.

By her university friends, Stanley Ann is remembered talking for hours about philosophy in coffee shops, always challenging, always arguing.

She was considered that most disagreeable of female creatures in those days: a contrarian. She was also an initial rejecter of organized religion, in short not one for the 'accepted version' or 'business-as-usual'.

In other words, Stanley Ann was Woman As Iconoclast.

She had been named after her father because he had wanted a son so badly.

She had to deal with a 'funny name' as a child.

Just like her son.

Obama's mother spent 8th grade through highschool in the Pacific Northwest, in Seattle.

She was a typical girl in many ways: she worried about her weight, rolled her eyes when her parents said what she considered to be stupid things etc.

But she tried always to listen to herself and live her own life, not anyone else's.

While it is said that her put downs could be scorching, she did not like to draw attention to herself.

Above all, Dr. Stanley Ann Dunham sought all of her life to bridge divides, heal wounds, tell the truth as she saw it.

Barack Obama is his mother's son.

He is also the grandson of Stanley Armour Dunham.

In fact, to my mind, he is a Dunham pretty much through and through.

Take a look at a photo of his grandfather as a young man. Obama looks exactly like him: the same long chin with the crease almost at the base, same head shape, the same smile, along with his mother's straight, dark, low brows – his sister Maya has these brows, too.

Obama states that his 'Gramps' (an All-American Kansas nickname if there ever was one) liked to rebuild himself, readjust the tale.

'Gramps' sounds to me like a Wily Loman, that iconic character in Arthur Miller's classic masterpiece about the pursuit and loss of the American Dream: *Death Of a Salesman*.

Like Loman ('wiley low-man') there were times that 'Gramps' lived on a 'shoe-shine and a smile.'

He kept his young grandson steady, sheltered, protected.

However, he helped bring the young Obama up in Hawaii, where it was easier to have a black grandson, where existence was more multi-cultural, more 'coloured'.

It is through him that Obama is related, some times removed, to such people as the actor Robert Duval, Wallis Simpson, Harry Truman, perhaps even Brad Pitt, and most definitely to former Vice President Dick Cheney.

In the end, we are all six degrees of separation.

Ann Dunham has no ambiguity about how her son will be perceived in the world and how he must proceed.

She gives him photos of the black great and good. She shows him photos of struggle, of young people not much older than himself being harassed by snarling Alsatians, high-powered hoses, surrounded by faces of hate.

As a result of her encouragement, he will go on to read the masters: Richard Wright; Langston Hughes; James Baldwin; W.E.B. Dubois; Ralph Ellison, Malcolm X – particularly fascinated by the latter's transformation.

Malcom had been the leading light of the Nation of Islam, known as 'The Black Muslims.'

The 'Nation' was rapidly becoming the religion of choice for young black people in the urban areas, and for the incarcerated.

But gradually Malcolm moved away from denouncing white people as the devil's spawn and turned toward working for peace and justice for all people – particularly the oppressed.

Because of this, he became one of the young Obama's touchstones.

But this is in the future.

Now, when he is still a little boy, Stanley Ann gives her son something gentler, yet just as strong: the music of Mahalia Jackson.

To listen to. To learn from.

If you lived and grew up on the South Side, the main gospel voice, arguably the only one, was that of Mahalia Jackson.

After years of struggle, she broke through with *Move On Up A Little Higher* at the end of the '40's, whose title my idol, James Baldwin, gave to his first semi-autobiographical novel about the boy preacher in Harlem.

We grew up on Ruby Avenue to *Go tell It On the Mountain*, a deep and rousing song that once heard can never be forgotten.

Mahalia can be heard and seen in the rousing church funeral finale of the gloriously over the top Douglas Sirk 1959 version of *Imitation Of Life*.

This film was the apogee of a series of films about black women who passed for white and had hell to pay for doing it: *Pinky* in 1949; *Kings Go Forth,* at the end of the '50's; *I Passed For White* at the beginning of the '60's.

These films starred white actresses playing black women passing for white.

In fact the only black woman who ever played a black woman posing as a white woman was in the original 1930's *Imitation Of Life*: the magnificent Fredi Washington.

With her white skin and green eyes Washington actually looked whiter than the white actresses who played black women passing for white (Are you keeping up?!). She was begged by her agent to actually do it for real and pass for white so that she could get work, not only did Washington totally refuse, but she became a fighter for greater racial equality in the movie industry, as well as a prominent journalist and stalwart member of New York's black community.

There you have it – the madness – white actors playing black characters passing for white, and a black actor who could have passed for white nobly, and fatally for her career, refusing to do so.

All part of the racial addiction/pathology that is my native land

And all very bizaare for us kids who watched these films on late night tv and thought them pretty hilarious. ...deeply weird.

I had put Mahlia aside until I became flatmates in New York with my Chicago gay Italian friend who was obsessed with Mahlia, and from whom I learned what a great woman this gospel singer really was.

As usual, somebody outside of my community had to tell me where the jewels in the crown were.

It was Rickey who began each day in the West Village, dressed like Lucille Ball in *I Love Lucy,* singing Miss Jackson's beautiful *In The Upper Room* about being present at the Last Supper as he did his morning's ferocious cleaning.

This was the song at his funeral, too, at far too young an age.

A Message From Munich

In *The Audacity Of Hope*, Obama writes about watching the very rapid death from cancer of his brave, beloved mother.

He has spoken of how worried she was about her health insurance, if it could cover everything, of how she spent her time arguing with her insurance company, time she could have spent trying to get well.

America does have health care that is the envy of the world.

You just have to be able to access it.

For millions of people with no job that can provide a Plan, there is no primary care. You have to go to the emergency room for your toothache, your migraine, your twinge in the shoulder.

If you come to the Emergency Room, it is obliged, by law, to take care of you.

This pulls treatment away from real emergency care, drains the hospital of those who are genuinely sick, sends cost up and premiums up.

Upstairs in a hospital could look like a posh hotel, while the emergency room is like….think of the *Titanic* and that about sums it up.

He has written that she was afraid, and lonely, too.

Trained as an anthropologist, an observer of the journey, she would have no way of chronicling this last voyage, of telling others what she had observed, what she had felt, her conclusions.

She could no longer collect, in her beloved cloth, testaments in woof and warp of a people's inner life, of their yearning, their joy, their approach to the things of this world, and to the divine.

I am listening to Sam Cooke on radio one afternoon, when a phone call comes in.

It is from an old childhood friend from Ruby Avenue.

She has been travelling with her husband for the first time in Europe.

I expect her to tell me that they have arrived at our place in Nice.

But no.

It's to tell me that her husband has just had a heart attack in their Munich hotel and can I please come over right away.

She can't speak a word of German and doesn't know what's going on.

I sit still for a moment. I feel like fainting. This is one of my best and dearest friends. I've known her all of my life.

I ring a close friend in Paris whose wife is German. She rings the hospital in Munich to find out what's going on. He's being prepped for emergency surgery.

She rings my friend to tell her what is happening.

My husband, who speaks a bit of German, talks to the hospital too, at the same time as we look for flights.

I'm numb.

Somehow I arrive in Munich and the taxi driver knows right where I have to go. It is to one of the finest heart hospitals in Europe. Yeltsin had been treated there. If anybody can help my friends, they can.

I arrive at the doors of the hospital and run inside.

It is silent, empty, you can eat off the floors it's so clean.

I run to my friend.

She, who is so confident, always so radiant, looks like a child in shock. I almost scream when I first see her, but I hold it in.

No one speaks English and her husband is in surgery, on the table.

We wait.

She prays aloud.

I don't know what to do but just be there.

It seems like an eternity passes until the young doctor walks out to us.

His face is grave.

Bill has made it, but it was a close run thing.

He must have angels around him, the doctor says. He has never seen anyone survive anything like this.

He had had a massive heart attack.

Lisa collapses.

She tells me, after we have a drink of water and sit down to wait until Bill goes into intensive care, that as soon as she realised what was happening, she rang the hotel desk.

They in turn rang the hospital, and an ambulance was there within minutes. They stabilized him in the hotel room and then took him down through the window with the help of the fire department which had also come along.

The doctor returns to sit with us.

We talk about Chicago, a place he wants to see.

Then he says that one thing really perplexed him through all of this: they had a hard time settling Bill down.

He kept reciting his insurance number, wondering if his insurance covered what was happening to him.

The doctor had tried to tell him that he was only concerned about saving his life, that he didn't know anything about money and didn't care, either. But Bill couldn't deal with that until he couldn't fight any longer and went under.

A few hours later we see him in intensive care.

He asks what has happened.

Lisa gently tells him. Bill stops her and tells her that he can't listen to anymore. He falls asleep.

We return to their room.

Then the real nightmare begins.

It takes us a week to get any action form their HMO – their local medical whatever.

First, nobody can understand about Munich.

What part of the States is it located in.

That hurdle passed, we then have to find out if Bill is covered and how to get him home.

In America, the reality is that Bill's bill for a month in hospital, which is what he needs just to get him to where he can begin treatment, could easily come to a million dollars.

You have pay for EVERYTHING including the water you drink and the glass you drink it from.

Yes, health care is excellent, superb in many cases, but if you don't have a job or the right policy, you're a right-off.

And even if you have everything in place, God only knows what you might have to pay up front before the insurance kicks in.

And that is if Bill's condition is not genetic or in existence before his heart attack.

If it is, forget it.

Goodbye house, the whole shooting match.

As we wait for San Francisco to wake up, I think of the NHS back in Britain.

Say what you will, complain all you like, but one thing's for sure: in Britain, I don't believe that anyone resists anaesthesia because they're afraid their medical insurance is not in place.

One afternoon, after 10 hour days on the phone, Lisa and I go outside to a café and have a coffee with some cognac in it.

We need it.

Good old Munich.

Good old Europe.

Good old National Health Service

We're drunk now.

We deserve it.

Lisa says that health care is THE human right all Americans should have.

NOT owning guns.

We drink to that, Bill's health and lots of other stuff, and find ourselves listening to the radio inside the café on the bar.

It is Quincy Jones' part gospel version of Handle's *Messiah*.

We sing along.

We don't give a monkeys.

It's a damn good day.

It is very difficult for us in Europe to fully understand the maelstrom that is the American health care debate.

But if the President can win this one, and pass his Plan, he will truly transform American society and go a long way toward lowering its high rate of obesity and infant mortality.

The stakes are high; it is expensive; more doctors will have to be trained; insurance companies may not be able to compete with the Federal government and therefore go out of business; there may be a degree of 'socialization' on the same level as Medicare, for example; Americans may have to become less dependant on pills because it will no longer be lucrative to turn out so much medication.

(The highest cause of liver failure in the US is... aspirin!).

There can be no question that health reform in the US is necessary. All sides agree.

But how, and to what extent?

But if anyone can bring that reform about, this President can.

On The Hill

The beginning of July, The G8 Conference.
Barack Obama, the newly elected 44th President of the United States, has arrived in Rome for a conference with the most powerful nations on earth.

President Berlesconi is looking forward to again muscling in on the young President's status as most famous man on the planet. Earlier in the year, in London, the Italian head of state had even managed to cause the usually un-ruffled Elizabeth Two to make the equivalent of a 'what's up with him?' retort that went viral on YouTube.

This is the high summer of Obama's popularity, the arc of his fame.

A particularly feverish blogger makes the point that the President has a lot in common with the Roman Emperor Lucius Septimius Severus. Hadn't anyone noticed besides him?

It was all there: the African father, the white mother, the clever, driven wife, his own war in Mesopotamia complete with surge and a triumphal arch in Rome to commemorate it.

On Ruby Avenue, growing up, I had two best friends, two

women that I have come to see reflected the two sides of me. One was cerebral, scholarly, shy, a dreamer and a wanderer. Cynthia.

Cynthia was a scholar, a linguist, a fellow bookworm, and her parents had great ambitions for her.

She was the only girl and the baby of the family.

Her health was delicate, as I was to come to know, but she never allowed that to stop her. She was captain of the soccer team at school, a great honour in a game that is still considered in the States to be for girls.

Her family lived in a bungalow similar to ours, part of a street of houses built between the wars for people who definitely were not us.

Cynthia's father made cars on an assembly line, risking his life in an ethic white neighbourhood – like our father did – at risk from people who only had the colour of their skin to distinguish and elevate themselves above our economic lot.

When he could, he parked cars at some big hotel downtown so that his children could attend Catholic schools, the working class black man's gateway to a halfway decent education for his children.

Her mother was friendly, always at home, baking, cleaning, like my mother, the very incarnation of the word 'housewife.'

It looked like a doomed life to me.

Nevertheless our mothers made us secure girls because we always felt that we had a home to return to.

While my other siblings were outgoing, I was an introvert, and Cynthia was, too.

We would read books together in her quiet house and talk

about our dreams.

Our dreams quite simply were about other places, places far away from Ruby Avenue, and the South Side.

We loved the movies but could not imagine ourselves as movie stars or politicians or artists. No one in those categories looked like us. But somehow we dared to imagine ourselves as adventurers.

It didn't matter that the life we wanted could not possibly be imagined by our parents nor our ancestors.

We would have it.

In time, I became distracted, unfocussed by my romantic nature and natural impatience, but Cynthia stayed the course – through highschool and on to university to study ethnology.

Her goal was to make visible what was invisible, to live where she could not live, be what she could not be.

She wanted to live in the Sahara, get to know the peoples, learn their languages, their way of being.

One of her theories was that our restlessness had to do with our being descended from the Fulani people, the desert people, who crossed the Sahara to Senegal, Mali, Ghana, and in time became us.

One summer, while I was working in a downtown bank to pay my university fees, she was in Rome perfecting her Italian and writing her thesis.

She was sharing a tiny apartment on the Aventine Hill, one of the seven hills of Rome.

The Aventine, she had written, was very beautiful, full of lovely houses and lovely trees and I dreamt about it while handling nasty bank notes behind my cage in the cold bank.

I ate Campbell's soup and was grateful.

Cynthia grew basil in flower pots on her window sill and cooked it in her fresh pasta.

She had known, she wrote, that she had done the right thing because when she walked into the apartment, her new flatmate was playing a record by The Staple Singers, who had, from time to time, sung at her grandmother's church: the mighty Pilgrim Baptist Church.

It was difficult to grow up on the South Side in the '60's without knowing about Pilgrim and the Staple Singers and Albertina Walker and James Cleveland.

Pilgrim Baptist was once a synagogue, designed by the premier architects of Chicago's 'robber baron' age of the 1890's: Sullivan and Adler.

It is called the birthplace of gospel. Thomas Dorsay was director of music there, and in the fullness of time, everyone who was anyone sang there and preached there, including Martin Luther King.

Jack Johnson, the great black boxer, was buried there,

In 2006 the church almost burned down, but the walls are intact and there is a fund raising drive.

Albertina Walker is a 'Queen Of Gospel' not only because of her prodigious output and many awards, but because of 'The Caravans', a group she founded which featured such legends as Shirley Caesar and Loleata Holloway whose soul record *Right On Time* was a UK Number One in the '80's.

Ms. Walker's *Mary, Don't You Weep* was one of those gospel records that graced my childhood and which you could hear issuing from every house on Ruby Avenue from time to time.

James Cleveland, who had worked with Miss Walker, became one of the driving forces behind the modern gospel sound, and recorded a version of Ray Charles' *Hallelujah I Love her So* at the end of the '50's which became a great hit. He developed large, disciplined groups which mastered complex orchestrations – the sound of today.

The Staple Singers began singing in churches at the end of the '40's.

Roebuck 'Pops' Staples was the shining light of the group, born in Mississippi like so many of our parents had been. He and his children in time created their masterpiece: *I'll Take you There* and *Respect Yourself*, pure r'n'b, but always with their pristine gospel harmonies driving the music.

That summer for Cynthia was gospel in Rome and the Aventine was perfect – Italian men whispering '*bella*' to her, and there was simply the sheer beauty of Rome.

The Via Veneto was still as mad as it is depicted in the film *La Dolce Vita* and she had met an Italian boy who was teaching her to ride a Vespa.

They would speed through the city when he wasn't busy trying to get inside of her clothes, and he introduced her to the great churches of Rome, churches I saw, too, through her letters.

The one closest to her on the Aventine was called Saint Sabina's – Basilica di Santa Sabina all'Aventino – the same name as the church that one of her cousins belonged to back in Chicago, a church not far from Pilgrim Baptist.

That church is now the parish church of Father Michael Phleger, one of that courageous band of activist diocesan priests (priest ordained to work in Chicago parishes only) who from time to time defy their bishops in the service of what they believe to be right.

Activist priests are a strong tradition in Chicago and on the South Side.

Father Pheleger has worked with Jesse Jackson, Louis Farrakhan and Jeremiah Wright, former pastor of President Obama.

Under him St. Sabina's has shut down shops selling drug paraphernalia; bought time from prostitutes so that they could get counselling; taken on Jerry Springer's talk show; attacked 'negative' rappers; protested against the mostly white athletic organization 'Southside Catholic Conference'; took on gun shop owners; and most controversially Father Pheleger stated a very strong opinion regarding the then Presidential candidate Hillary Clinton which made national news and earned him a short leave of absence from his parish.

This was a priest whose roots were in the '60's, when Cynthia and I had begun to see that our way forward would have to be different from that of our parents', different from those who were only a decade older than us.

Son Of Man

Vatican Two, the Council set up by Pope John The Twenty Third
to open up the Catholic Church to the modern world, had begun
to introduce a Christ and a Bible which spoke to the liberation of
oppressed people, something the South Side heard and acted
upon.

This Vatican Two Jesus became the Son Of Man, and out of all
of this emerged 'Black Liberation Theology.'

The Pastor in the church of one of my sister's, in summer of the
'08 campaign, in the heat of the Father Phelger and Reverend
Wright controversy, looked at his congregation and proclaimed: 'If
anybody in here is thinking of running for President, you gotta get
up and get outta here. This is a Negro church!'

This is what he meant:

Black Liberation Theology aims principally to liberate people
of African descent from what it considers to be oppression at every
level.

Its other intention is to liberate Christianity from its associations
with slavery, and to make it, instead, speak to what people trapped
in ghettos need: open housing; jobs; a better education etc.

Black Liberation Theology is neither passive nor nostalgic. It is active, and in the present. What God is doing, He's doing right now.

The American press – correctly or incorrectly – considers a church near Ruby Avenue – Trinity United Church of Christ – to be one of its international epicentre.

A few months after the birth of Barack Obama, a dozen South Siders met at a local elementary school next to Halstead Street.

The Nation Of Islam, particularly since its charismatic and articulate spokesman Malcolm X had begun doing the chat shows, was beginning to influence many South Siders.

The Christian community needed to find a way to address the same concerns, and when the new Trinity's plans to merge with a white congregation in order to create an integrated membership fell through – the white people did not want to come into the community – Trinity opened in my community just east of the colour line.

Gradually, as Trinity became more and more committed to the struggles and well-being of its community, it welcomed a new minister: the son of a minister; a holder of several degrees; and in 1966, as a U.S. Navy Hospital Corpsman, an assistant to President Lyndon Baines Johnson: one Rev. Jeremiah Wright.

President Obama has written in both his books about how much Trinity's now pastor emeritus has meant to him.

He named *The Audacity Of Hope* after one of Wright's sermons.

Obama found his Christian faith at Trinity under Wright; married Michelle there; had Malia and Sasha baptized right there at my local church.

Jeremiah Wright turned Trinity into a community force and a source of health, solace and justice, not only for South Siders, but for a young man from Hawaii trying to find himself and his place in the world.

Much has been written about Reverend Wright's controversial remarks during the '08 campaign which led the then candidate Obama to leave Trinity and distance himself from Wright.

As of this writing, the President has yet to find another church.

I can't assess that particular controversy, I don't have all the facts.

But these are a few facts that I do know:

Cynthia had decided to join the Peace Corps.

She had chosen to work in the Sahel, the often drought-stricken region below the Sahara.

All that we – her family, Ruby Avenue, me – know is that she was caught up in a dust storm during a terrible drought and died of an asthma attack in a village on the edge of the desert.

Because she had died abroad, the US would not allow her coffin to be opened for fear of contagion.

She was certified to be who her name tag said in Paris by the Peace Corps and after that shipped home.

Her death ended my girlhood, and I can remember sitting for hours with her picture in my lap, trying to imagine her last moments so far from home, so far from me.

I sat staring at her closed coffin at the base of the pulpit, silent, closed, so untypical of most black funerals where the coffin is often, and you can even kiss the face of the corpse. I kissed my dad's decades later.

I couldn't see because of the tears, couldn't breathe because of the grief.

It is impossible, when you're young, to understand how someone your age – your dearest friend – could be gone forever.

I tried to talk to her in my head, screaming for her to wake me up from this nightmare. I didn't think that I could continue to sit there in that church, when suddenly the new, young preacher stepped forward – Jeremiah Wright.

He said words that gave me a way quite simply to continue my life.

Jeremiah Wright allowed me to walk out onto that South Side street on an unreasonably sunny day with his gospel choir's songs ringing in my ear and his words embedded in my soul. They helped me to believe that someday, somewhere, somehow I would see my dear Cynthia once again.

A Change Is Gonna Come

The day before Sam Cooke was murdered, one of the nuns at our secondary school introduced us to the poetry of Gwendolyn Brooks.

It had been a harrowing year for the handful of us black girls at the school. John F. Kennedy had been assassinated during our morning assembly and so, for an hour, we had known nothing about it. Then we were sent home immediately and I can still see people crying in the streets on my short walk back across the colour line to Ruby Avenue.

We were all just at the beginning of adolescence and had no idea that we were living in a decade of death – even the death of some of our friends.

All of the ferocious South Side gangs were to the east and the north of us, not yet a reality in our neighbourhood. The community knew of them, but was not yet part of them.

Our father had moved us to the South Side to escape gang activity on the West Side, but there was no tranquility amongst the bungalows, and the hedges and fruit trees. We were subject to random racist attacks from whites afraid that we were moving closer and closer to their communities and would thus destroy their way of life.

Born in Kansas, Miss Brooks was brought to Chicago as a baby, so therefore was one of us.

She had chosen one of the hardest jobs there is, that of a poet and she wanted to express her people. She had lived in a kitchenette with her family at first, the sort of place where so many of us had started life, and she had eventually written *A Street In Bronzeville* which led to the Pulitzer Prize, the first black person ever to win.

Only two years before the moment we were introduced to Brooks, President Kennedy had awarded her a medal.

We read bits of the beautiful *Annie Allen*, and it gave us black girls a great deal of pride to see ourselves in poetry.

I also liked:

THE BALLAD OF RUDOLPH REED
The agent's steep and steady stare
Corroded to a grin.
Why you black old, tough old hell of a man,
Move your family in!

But we were all shell-shocked still from the death of Kennedy.

We had seen him as some kind of emancipator, the only one we had known who had begun to effect change.

Now, what would happen?

We had seen Sam Cooke perform his song *A Change Is Gonna Come* on the *Tonight Show* with Johnny Carson, whom our mother loved and our father loathed. To him the song seemed like a set-up, a sop to the horror that had happened a few months earlier, but I think that our mother saw the song as a signal of the kind of hope everyone was looking for, and Sam had that beautiful Gospel voice.

A year or so later he was dead, just another example as far as our dad was concerned that there would be no change, no change whatsoever.

But I had Gwendolyn Brooks, and James Baldwin, which I read by flashlight under the covers after my sisters quieted down and went to sleep.

I couldn't figure out the world.

I didn't want to.

Sam had a huge funeral. I can recall lines of mourners around the block and I seem to recall a sea of white clothes and a South Side funeral home and the horror on all of the faces of the adults on Ruby Avenue – when would it stop?

Chicago was run by what was known as 'The Machine' – a tightly run organization of political patronage, corruption, back-slapping, Mafiosi and dirty Democrat dealings. The town worked like clock-work, particularly if you were part of the way it worked, and atop it sat a roly-poly bit of malevolence know as Richard J. Daley, known fondly or not as 'da mayor'.

In fact he had been mayor so long that I had grown into my ado-lescence thinking that this was his first name.

He was a South Sider, too, from what were known as the 'Back Of The Yards', a tough, working-class Irish community.

Being from that community, I figured that the mayor had to have known something about the infamous Regan's Colts who figured prominently in the terrorizing of the black community.

After Dr. King was assassinated in 1968, the South Side exploded. The Chicago Police had been accused of being too soft on the black community, which had expressed its grief by burning parts of itself down.

Jesse Jackson, a young preacher who had been present when Dr. King was killed, had come to Chicago three years before that tragedy to carry on his work and push it forward to another level.

He helped to set up a branch of Dr. King's Southern Christian Leadership Conference (SCLC) in 1965, after the historic Selma to Montgomery Alabama marches for freedom.

He also set up 'Operation Breadbasket' on the South Side whose goal was to 'selectively buy' or boycott as a way to pressurize white businesses to buy from black contractors and to do business with black people in general.

Before that, he had been successful in organising boycotts against Southern rest stops that would not cater to black people.

In 1968, in Chicago, Rev. Jackson set up 'Operation PUSH' (People United To Save Humanity) and later 'The National Rainbow Coalition' which grew out of Jesse's 1984 presidential campaign; all from the south Side, all from our powerful city, national and international organizations dedicated to helping the poor and working class, organisations whose networks and links are formidable.

Reverend Jackson is first and foremost a preacher and his language is the language of the church. But by the late '60's, exhaustion and the rage had begun to set in. The Church, although formidably organized with an extensive network, felt too slow, too accommodating, and if singing gospel tunes right before we did anything was the way it would be, the young wanted no part.

Meanwhile native South Sider Harold Washington, after a stint in service in World War Two, had graduated from law school at the beginning of the '50's and set to work with Ralph Metcalf. Together with the former Olympic athlete, who had run in the Berlin Games with Jesse Owen and had defeated Hitler's supermen, he was attempting to defeat the power structure of Chicago politics.

Harold had terms in the state legislature and Congress, during which he worked tirelessly to forge change in the electoral system and to encourage the engagement of black people and working people with their politics.

One writer states that Washington even used the word 'Kafkaesque' to describe Chicago politics, the fact that a Chicago politician might also read literature was mind boggling to that particular writer.

In 1983, Harold won the Democratic nomination for mayor after a titanic struggle against elements of his own Party, this nomination effectively electing him mayor in this safely Democrat city.

In *Dreams From My Father* Barack Obama writes of his third day back in Chicago.

He's sitting in 'Smitty's', all around the barbershop are photos of the late mayor of Chicago, Harold Lee Washington.

On his way he had noticed Mayor Washington's smiling face everywhere, in the shops owned by Arabs and Koreans, but above all, in the window of every establishment he had seen on the South Side.

The barber is telling him how it was on election day, the election of the first black mayor in one of the most racially segregated cities in the nation: people had come out to vote in droves, and after Washington had won, they had taken to the streets.

Everyone had felt that they were experiencing a personal victory, as if they were all going to church at the same time.

The old barber tells Obama that it was like the day Joe Louis knocked out Max Schmeling – a day to forget the disrespect, the abuse.

Harold had lived on the South Side, too, as Mayor, a real son come home.

Living in New York on the day of Harold's election, Obama had felt the pride, too, of Washington's win.

Obama listens, wondering if he could, someday, become the second black man elected mayor of this mighty city.

Obama had applied to work with Washington, but was rejected. Nevertheless, he resolved to somehow work with him, as he writes in *Dreams*: he needed to be noticed by him.

Washington's election was a huge psychological and political boost for the black community.

Washington did not live downtown, but on the South Side, in the community.

The usually reliable white voters in the Party deserted for the Republicans, believing that this black man would bring in 'gang-bangers' from the South Side to run government.

The mayor had to govern by veto for most of his first term while he helped to build a strong base in the black community, along with its allies, a base that would bring change to Chicago politics.

In fact, Washington himself WAS the change, as he demonstrated by being voted in for a second term, this time bringing whites along with him without altering his progressive programs of civic, educational and environmental improvement, while promoting reform in the police department through the Afro American Patrolmen's league.

He, who had been a part of the Machine, and had discovered that to effect change he would have to find his way out of that Machine, had done what many had thought impossible: demonstrate to the citizenry at large that a black person could govern a major city.

In 1987,the Wednesday after Thanksgiving, that holiday when families come together and reconciliations are made, Harold collapsed at his desk while talking to his press secretary about education reform. He never regained consciousness.

I loved Harold.

In Lisa Mundy's *Michelle A Biography* she writes that Obama would interrogate his new boss, in Chicago, a white public interest attorney, who had worked with Harold about what it was like to work for a black man, how he had felt.

He needed to know if it could happen, if it was possible.

Almost eight years after his death, Obama shared his views about Harold with Hank de Zutter from the mighty *Chicago Reader*: 'Washington was the best of the classic politicians. He knew his constituency; he truly enjoyed people. That can't be said for a lot of politicians. He was not cynical about democracy and the democratic process – as so many of them are. But he, like all politicians, was primarily interested in maintaining his power and working the levers of power... He was a classic charismatic leader...and when he died all of that dissipated. This potentially powerful collective spirit that went into supporting him was never translated into clear principles, or into an articulable agenda for community change.

'The only principle that came through was 'getting our fair share,' and this runs itself out rather quickly if you don't make it concrete. How do we rebuild our schools? How do we rebuild our communities? How do we create safer streets? What concretely can we do together to achieve these goals?

'When Harold died, everyone claimed the mantle of his vision and went off in different directions. All that power dissipated.

''Now an agenda for getting our fair share is vital. But to work, it can't see voters or communities as consumers, as mere recipients or beneficiaries of this change. It's time for politicians and other leaders to take the next step and to see voters, residents, or citizens as producers of this change. The thrust of our organising must be on how to make them productive, how to make them employable, how to build our human capital, how to create businesses, institutions, banks, safe public spaces – the whole agenda of creating productive communities. That is where our future lies.

'The right wing talks about this but they keep appealing to that old individualistic bootstrap myth: get a job, get rich, and get out. Instead of investing in our neighbourhoods, that's what has always happened. Our goal must be to help people get a sense of building something larger.

'The political debate is now so skewed, so limited, so distorted…. People are hungry for community; they miss it. They are hungry for change.'

I like to see Harold's mayoralty as gospel, as jubilee, that testament to a higher power, that belief in it too.

He and his supporters had started for the mountaintop, and had reached it too, until fate had sent them down from it.

But Harold had changed the landscape. Things in Chicago would never be the same again.

Barack extends Harold's work, deepens it.

In *Dreams From My Father*, Barack writes about Harold coming to see his community project, not noticing the young community organiser.

But the young community organiser had noticed him, and was learning.

Because of the spirit he engendered and the love and power that he helped black Chicagoans in particular continue to cultivate and activate, it is safe to say that if Harold Washington had not been elected the first black mayor of Chicago – there would be no President Barack Obama.

SOUL

Signed, Sealed, Delivered

Memphis Soul

Mid July, 2009.
President of the United States, Barack Obama is addressing the
NAACP: The National Association for the Advancement of
Colored People, one of the oldest and arguably the most important
Civil Rights organization in the United States and therefore on
planet Earth.

The mission of the NAACP is to eliminate racial discrimination
everywhere and it has finally happened: a President of African
descent is finally standing up before them.

They are dressed in their very best and what a proud, unbeliev-
able moment this is, at this, their organization's 100th convention.

Obama takes the podium, his face beaming.

He begins with the historic rise of the organization, the valour
of its leaders, how their sacrifice and hard work and struggle made
it possible for him to stand before them. He also points out that the
racial barriers still persist.

There are still the gangs, the horrific poverty, poor educational
provision…but….

And then he lets them have roughly the same deal that he had
delivered the week before in Accra: 'I-Know-the-Problems-But-
It's-Up-To-You-At-The-End-Of-The-Day-I-Don't-Want-To-Hear-

About-The-White-Man-Anymore-Hardship-Will-Make-You-Stronger-Yes-We-Can-Thank-You-Very-Much.'

The following evening on American cable television, the commentator's only observation is to wonder aloud why his accent seems so different from the way he speaks in the Rose Garden, and do other people from Honolulu talk that way.

Maybe the South Side has something to do with it.

South Side directness is wrapped up in soul and that directness has a certain sang froid, a certain bluntness that earlier on got Michelle Obama criticised when she talked about her husband's morning breath and other human foibles.

South Side soul is a cousin of Memphis Soul so let's start our examination there.

Memphis is on the road to Chicago, and its citizens are as much a part of the South Side community as those native born.

None of us could imagine South Side soul without Isaac Hayes, Wilson Pickett, Otis Reddng, Al Green, The Staples, the Bar-Keys and Staxx Records.

It was to take its place alongside the Chicago sounds of Jerry Butler and Curtis Mayfield, with its stomping optimism, belief in its own self and its own way.

Its glistening self-confidence is the sound the President would have heard in the highways and byways of the South Side.

Memphis met Chicago at some moment in the early '60's, around the time of the President's birth.

Watching Water

Barack Obama is facing his destiny.

It is the end of the '80's.

He is deciding whether to stay in New York City and live a life of relative comfort, the kind of life that a graduate of several posh schools would be entitled to expect.

Or go west. To Chicago.

He is sitting and thinking as he watches the East River.

He writes about the moment when a little black boy, watching the river too, his mother beside him, asks Obama why it runs one way, then the other.

Obama tells him that it must have something to do with the tides.

But he suddenly realizes that he has never asked himself that question.

He has never thought about the East River.

He has never really lived in New York.

A week later he packs his car and drives to Chicago and to the rest of his life.

He is heading to my hometown.

To the city they call 'The Go'.

I lived in New York City, too, all over Manhattan – uptown, midtown, downtown, and on the West Side, the Village, Brooklyn, and I loved it.

I even got that New York withdrawal, when you are away from The Apple for a few days and you suddenly start wondering what's going on there, what are you missing. Because you are missing something, if you're away from New York.

But I'd never really thought about those rivers either.

I've never dreamed about the Hudson or the East River, or going down to the Battery and standing at the water's edge.

But Lake Michigan, well, I'd think about that a lot. I still do.

An actor friend born in Trinidad told me once, after he had first seen it that it had reminded him of the sea.

The lake is beautiful and big and blue, and it is also treacherous.

Not the lake so much itself, but the fact that it wasn't always a welcoming place for black people.

Now you can live on it or near it with practically no fear.

The Obamas live near it.

My aunt can see it out of the window of her senior citizen's building.

It's icy and stark in the blasts of winter.

But in the summer…

The summer.

The South Side of Chicago always exists in the summer to me.

There are the lawns, assiduously mown and watered and fed every summer.

There are the backyards, refuges in the heat of the summer.

Some are patios, paved and carefully put together with elaborate furniture, some of the furniture so elaborate that the patios of my childhood and youth looked like nothing more than South

Side's versions of Versailles' *Petit Trianon*.

Some of the backyards had gardens, gardens of flowers, or gardens of vegetables.

The vegetable gardens always touched me because they reminded me of the Southern rural heritage of so many of the people in the community I grew up in.

My part of the South Side is about arching sprinklers that made the lawns perpetually green.

When I was a child, I did not know the price my parents and every black parent in our neighbourhood paid to have a house, to be there.

I played in our family backyard with my other brothers and sisters.

I would sit on the front step with one of my two best friends talking about the great world that we wanted to enter someday.

Once, as I sat and stared at the column of water that arched over the cars and the children who played in that water, I remembered the first time that I had gone down south.

I must have been three.

I can remember the smell of heavily spiced cold fried chicken in a cardboard shoebox, the lunch that our mother had prepared for us.

I can remember sitting on the cramped seats, my baby brother on Mama's lap, our father sitting opposite us, my sister Lelia eleven months younger than me and a genuine Daddy's girl, sitting very close to Daddy.

I can remember eating the chicken, how cold it was, but it didn't matter. It was made by Mama.

I can remember the South being lots of dust with chickens playing in it and sitting on a stair with my feet moving around in the dirt, and a slow, old lady, her beige skin glowing in the heat, standing in the afternoon gloom of a room full of old photos and beautiful wallpaper, wallpaper decorated in flowers.

The woman was my father's mother, also called Lelia, whom I never really knew.

She died shortly after our visit, and my mother tells me that as my father lay dying, he would occasionally smile through his pain because, he said to her, he could see her – his mother – standing in that doorway in Mississippi.

Years later I learned that our train on that journey had been a segregated one, like everything in those days. It was the mid '50's and we had had to ride in the front, the dirtiest part – near the engine. We would not have been allowed to eat in the dining car. No Negroes. Even if a relative had been working as a porter on the train, we would not have seen him.

He wouldn't have been in our section.

But I was a child then, barely out of babyhood and completely unaware of these things, unaware of the change and the turmoil in those days when America was being forced to confront its own *raison d'etre*.

And unaware of the part that the city of my birth – Chicago – and the South Side itself had in all of this.

This very link to the South – the dust and the chickens, the shoe-boxes full of food and our home created soul music itself.

The Closer

Soul and r'n'b can often seem trivial, lightweight, not worthy of thought and certainly not of analysis.

After all, what can be said about 'ooh, baby, baby'; or 'I want you back' followed by screams and shouts?

Soul and r'n'b can be dismissed as background music, the cheap and cheerful accompaniment to something not quite up to snuff.

But it's called 'soul' simply because it's dredged up from deep inside, from deeper inside than the blues, or gospel or jazz.

Soul is primal, and its lyrics are merely a façade, a covering for that which cannot be named.

A great soul song encompasses experience and the landscape of dreams. It masks these in a dance beat, and if you like, you can completely ignore it, dismiss it, laugh at it.

Soul came into being simply because there was no better way to express the urban reality that black people faced, particularly in Chicago, where some say, soul music found its purest and truest expression.

If you sang the blues all day you would eventually wind up face down, floating down the Lake, or heading for the pavement from the tallest building in the Loop. Soul took the same feelings, the same reality and point of view, and made it possible to live on earth with them.

Its surface is jolly and danceable, but its 'soul' is profound and moving.

At its core, soul, Chicago soul, South Side soul simply speaks the truth. Beneath its furbelows and carapaces, it is plain spoken and direct.

'What you see is what you get' and 'down to the nitty-gritty' are soul expressions.

You grow up if you want to do soul.

Soul is the South Side. We breathe it in our air. And it is always with us, how close to the surface depends on circumstance and the whim of the gods.

You never know when it will rear its head and start to speak its truth.

I think now that the most controversial thing I have ever said on air or written was to question the very curious propensity of British women to refer to themselves as 'girls.'

Women long past girlhood insist upon this.

To not live in girldom, to not understand girlhood, to not glory in its various permutations, is not to understand something essential and fundamental about the British.

There is always a huge controversy raging about the absence of older women on television. No one talks about the fact that: British culture does not actually like women at all, not grown-up, fully-paid up adults of the female species; and women themselves collude sometimes in this gynophobia, for whatever gain baffles me.

I once asked the late Robin Cook why British society was this way and he said it was because Englishmen did not go to school with women, did not socialize with women, or as an Oxbridge former boyfriend of mine once called females: "those other chaps".

Could it be that simple?

Needless to say this is all quite alien to a South Sider.

And it is also precisely why Michelle Obama is emphatically not a 'girl'.

Therefore she really can't be described in the girly gush you read in the tabloids and broadsheets that passes too often for Michelle-analysis:

'… no drab pantsuits…she knows that a pencil skirt and cardi is often a girl's best friend'; ''let's not forget that she is black and worked her way up from a poor Chicago childhood…(which explains) her obvious pleasure in bling;' 'Obama seems not to have the need to remind others constantly of her intellect…she is comfortable with girl talk…'; 'there's plenty of eye contact, but of a slightly challenging nature...'; '...I was taking the tube at the beginning of rush hour…dressed very Michelle Obama: cropped jeans, vest, sneakers…my arms could do with a bit of work….'.

No.

A girl is Bridget Jones: miserable, apologetic and like the song goes: 'scared of livin' and 'fraid of dyin''.

Girls are nice and loyal to one another, but beneath that can be cattiness and fear, armed with an either covert or overt all-elbows approach to getting the best bargains before it's too late.

Girls complain.

They complain about age discrimination, for example, but only over a chardonnay with other girls. They are suckers for all things 'new', the 'latest', etc.

They fall for anti-ageing creams; botox parties; pants to make their behinds look smaller; celebrity gossip.

But if you don't have one 'girl' in your life, or lose that in your-self, you will lose something that has to do with vulnerability and a kind of damaged innocence.

These are things that should belong to all women, but for many South Side women – many black women – these 'girlish' qualities are qualities seldom allowed to flourish except sometimes at home and in church.

A South Sider is brought up to consider the word 'girl', as applied to women of a certain age, as an insult.

This goes back to the days of enslavement and long after that, when no matter how old, how distinguished you became, a black woman was always a 'girl'.

Downtown, in the 'Loop', the central part of Chicago, black people were a rarity or non-existent when I was growing up in the 60's.

If you entered a big department store – if they let you in – you were openly followed, as opposed to surreptitiously followed as some establishments do today.

One morning, my aunt took me to Marshall Fields,that late great department store, we walked up to the gloves counter and asked to see a pair.

I don't know what happened, but the next moment my rather fiery Mississippi aunt told the sales woman in no uncertain terms that she was not to refer to her (my aunt) as a 'girl'.

The woman was taken aback, but stood her ground, and if it weren't for a much older black woman who gently encouraged us to move on, we would have probably been handed over to the tender mercies of the Chicago Police Department.

I had never seen my aunt quite that angry before, and later, safely back on the South Side, over an ice cream soda at a shop under the 'L', she told me about the years of humiliation she had suffered, all because of the word 'girl.'

I pointed out that I had often heard her and my mother call one another girl.

She quickly explained that what they called one another was 'gurl', an altogether different word.

And concept

A gurl lives her life and she starts doing that pretty young.

The great soul singer, Chaka Khan, another South Side gurl who lives in London, is a prime example.

There were many self-styled and actual Yoruba priests on the South Side from the mid-sixties on, and one of them christened the young Yvette Marie Stevens Chaka Adunne Aduffe Yemoja Hodarhi Karifi'.

Chaka was a part of the AffroArts Theatre scene in the '60's.

She also volunteered for the Black Panthers Free Breakfast For Children program, a great soul refuge when I volunteered there.

The 'jams' blared on the record player in the room where the cooks made the breakfast for poor children from the surrounding housing estates, who came to get the only decent meal many of them would have that day.

The charismatic young head of the Chicago Black Panthers, Fred Hampton, would gently tell the kiddies over their grits and sausages that their fight was not a racial one but a class one.

In those days, Chaka was known to all of us and at quite a young age, too.

An apocryphal story is told that she once came out on the baseball field at her South Side high-school, and through the sheer brilliance of her voice, caused her team to win.

To my mind, all of Khan's genius meets in the perfect receptacle of *Ain't Nobody*, a real 'Go' song in spirit and drive.

She can sing the blues. But Chaka is soul.

And so is Michelle.

Michelle is the good little sister in one of Pam Grier's *Coffee* films who waits sedately but hopefully, locked away in some gangster's lair, while big sis is out there looking for her.

And none too gently.

In one of Pam's classic scenes, she is confronted by a very disagreeable white woman.

The white woman confronts her with: "I've got a black belt in karate so don't put your ugly face in my way."

Pam pauses. Picks up a bar stool and beats the white girl all over the bar.

The girl tries to get up. But Pam rather ungallantly and effectively beats her down again.

As the woman rolls around in her own blood, Pam says: "Yeah, and I got a black belt in bar stools!"

A gurl.

Whether Mom-In-Chief or organic vegetable gardener et al, a gurl does everything with soul.

She is what her husband calls her: "The Closer".

And when he first laid eyes on her at the law office they both worked at, he was, in the words of that Stevie Wonder song: 'signed, sealed, delivered.'

A gurl takes back seat to no one.

She rides beside her man in the triumph.

She is the one, as their chariot rolls along through the adoring crowd cheering, who whispers: '*Respica te, hominem te memento*' – 'Look behind you, remember, you are only a man.'

Beauty

Spring, 09.

POTUS and FLOTUS go on a date.

POTUS has promised this to FLOTUS and off they go.

They land in New York City for supper and later catch that late master of playwriting, August Wilson's greatest play, *Joe Turner's Come and Gone*.

The streets are cleared, and the press are travelling in their pack.

POTUS is dressed in his usual, laid-back casual elegance.

A blogger notes that FLOTUS is carrying something called a 'clutch'.

And also that FLOTUS looks very, very beautiful.

Exasperated by the perfection of it all, John Stewart, the satirist begs: 'Take it down a notch, dude!'

When I was a child, beauty was the most important thing to me.

As far as I was concerned, Latin Mass was the most beautiful; my soul music.

I had bullied everyone into getting baptized a few years before.

It gave us lower school fees and also, the Church to me was a wonderful place, full of great statues and incense, deep alcoves, flowers and bells.

It did perplex me that there was only one black face amongst the saints but I knew that sainthood took a long time, not the way it's fast-tracked today.

I collected the magazine of the Order that taught us – the Oblates – watching the progress of the postulants and novices, dreaming of one day wearing the white veil of the novice and being admitted into the community's august company.

I would practice walking around swinging my rosary from my side. None of this, of course, a contradiction in my mind with my cosmetics obsession and my crushes.

My crushes always extended to priests. Any woman – or man – out there who has a thing about priests knows how ridiculous and addictive this is.

You hear of a few lucky guys or gals who hit the bulls-eye and manage to end up luring some man away from his vows and setting up home, even having babies, but I'd never see myself running away with Father So-And-So. Mine was a bit like some sort of troubadour romance, something ethereal and ultimately doomed.

When they held the host up and said: 'This is my Body', ok, I knew it wasn't ok, I knew it wasn't THEIR body, but you can get mixed up sometimes.

Priest obsession fades after adolescence, then returns, I suspect after menopause.

I'm watching for the signs.

When Dr. King came to the West Side in the middle sixties in an effort to desegregate the appalling housing situation in Chicago, a phalanx of priests marched with him, very handsome, fit guys, I have to say, who had devoted themselves to God and to chastity.

Of course this is the attraction, but it's easy to fool yourself that it's something else.

I thought it was my need to talk about, what I was convinced was, my vocation with the visiting priests at our school.

We were desperately horny teenage girls, all of this damped down by the nuns as best they could. Whenever a male showed up in the vicinity, we went mad and there was a great stampede to see what the male looked like.

We were South Side girls and therefore a bit more forward than the ones on the posh near North Side, but not as all-out as West Siders.

Father McCallen showed up one morning. The poor guy was just coming around to do his pastoral duty.

The fashion then was for old-fashioned knickers, very Victorian complete with frilly bits and ribbon at the bottom. We all vied to see who had the most elaborate pair, which we demonstrated in the locker room each morning before class.

They say that when Miles Davis played in the old days, all of the ladies in the audience subtly parted their legs. On the day this young priest showed up to give us religious tuition, he was greeted by a sea of knickers.

We didn't do it on purpose. We weren't even aware of it actually. But this guy started blushing like crazy and couldn't stop as he tested us on the Apostolic Creed.

Our nun was shooting daggers out of her eyes, but she said nothing, not wishing, I guess, to draw attention to what was going on.

Poor old Father McCallen, a red-head with blue eyes, stuck around for the minimum of time, and then got the hell away from all that wild oestrogen splashing around.

Even though we had answered our questions and passed with flying colours, we all had detention to do. Writing out the Creed over and over again in our lined notebooks.

Two weeks later our class was taken to see a film called *The Cardinal*. It was an Otto Preminger movie with all of his typical heavy-handedness. The story was about a priest trying to find himself as he rises through the church hierarchy to the Vatican.

What I recall are the two things that obsessed me at the time: the plight of black people and the path of true love. They were one and the same to me.

To serve the former, in the movie, our hero priest journeys to the South where he tries to help the local black priest, with the black priest being flogged.

I don't remember our hero being beaten – he might have been – but the black priest was played by the late, great Ossie Davis so there was dimension in this minor character, but he still got flogged within an inch of his life. Maybe he died, too, which usually happened to good, nice black men in movies in those days, living up to Lennie Bruce's great question: "In a movie, what's the difference between a black man and Lassie? At the end Lassie lives."

And the love came in the form of the priest developing a passion for Romy Schneider who I think the Nazis get.

As we headed back to the South Side on our bus after the movie, the nun told us in no uncertain terms what we'd done to the poor priest.

I thought at the time that it had happened a while back and she still remembered it.

What's that old Buddhist story?

Two monks, who have taken a vow never to touch a woman, are walking along and reach a stream that they must cross. A woman is there and asks the monks to help her. One of the monks picks her up, carries her across, bids her "God speed" and they continue on their way.

Three or so hours later, the other monk says: "Brother. As you know, we are not allowed to touch women. We have taken a vow."

The other monk replies: "Brother, this is true. But I put the woman down hours ago."

The Du Bois Moment

Barack Obama is a young man, and this is his time of study.

He writes of his decision to take himself away, to try and come to grips with the identity that his wise mother knows his physiognomy won't let him escape.

One of the books that he picks up is *The Souls of Black Folk: Essays and Sketches* by W.E.Burghardt Du Bois, one of the most influential black-American thinkers of the 20th Century.

Du Bois's accomplishments are legion, and he is such a legend that when I was in Ghana, I stopped by his home. He had become a citizen of the country before he died.

Marcus Garvey, the great black advocate of self-empowerment, and some say a separatist,carried on a long feud with Du Bois, who considered him untenable.

Garvey referred to him as: 'purely and simply a white man's nigger' and 'a little Dutch, a little French, a little Negro... a mulatto... a monstrosity...'

I don't have access to what du Bois called him, but this 'monstrosity' would have been ideal for Obama to study as he made his journey to self-definition and self-discovery.

Du Bois' work implies the double consciousness in black America: a righteous anger and a drive to overcome the anger and turn the page.

The future President has sensed this, seen it, felt it in himself. But now he must study it, analyse it, think.

In a strange way, he is preparing himself for Chicago, where someone with his background would be looked upon suspiciously in the black community, a town where Garvey is revered in some circles as a secular saint (as is Du Bois).

You could say that they are brothers in synergy: Du Bois entered Harvard as an undergrad in 1888, Obama entered Harvard Law School in 1988.

The Souls of Black Folk, published in 1903, contains several essays on race, drawing on Du Bois' own life and work to take a look at the life of black people in America. The book is one of the early works of sociology.

For example, one of the chapters often cited as hugely influential, *Of the Faith of the Fathers*, looks at how deeply the black church is linked to black political movements.

Obama will learn this viscerally when he comes to Chicago to work as a community organiser.

In this essay, Du Bois argues that the Black Church is deeply connected to black political movements. Instead of seeing this as a positive, he sees this as a weakness that needs to be overcome. He sees the Church as the last remnant of tribal life that needs to be overthrown for Black Civilization to thrive. This is his analysis: that by the middle of the Eighteenth Century the black slave was at the bottom of the economic ladder. Because of this, he lost all natural joy in the world. The Church then offered him salvation in the next world, which he clung to. Du Bois says the Black Man must look to salvation in this life in order to build a culture of economic prosperity, in order to survive.

He offered a future program for the Church recommending

buying real estate for its members, and increasing their economic status in society.

Du Bois saw the necessity for an activist church – with soul.

Ooh, Child

It is the time following the birth of Barack and Michelle Obama's first child: Malia Ann.

In *Audacity*, Obama writes about those first months in the summer of 1998, when he and Michelle had the rare privilege of time together to be alone with their long-awaited first child.

All too soon he will have to return to the State legislature, Michelle will have to return to work, and the cracks in their relationship could open up again.

But for now, he is a new father, sitting with his infant child in their home, the stifling heat and humidity that is a Chicago summer enveloping them, feeding her, his child, feeling her breath against his cheek, and grateful that he and Michelle's natural rhythms are at last in synch: he can stay up with Malia at night – natural for him – while his wife sleeps.

In his book he writes about his baby daughter's eyes, about the wisdom in them.

She was born on the 4th of July. He has fathered a child in a nation that may not be ready for the gifts that she will bring to it.

A few miles further south of them and practically three decades earlier, Betty and Clarence Burke Sr's five children, known as The

Five Stairsteps are being hailed 'The First Family of Soul'.

Some of them had attended my highschool and we adored them. They were ours, special, local heroes, famous, feted, and in our imaginations undoubtedly rich.

Now they were growing in national stature.

They were burning up the airwaves, turning out covers versions and touring with mega Chi-town soul group, The Impressions.

I was much too bookish and shy to make friends with them at school, but in my own way, I shared in their success. They, and the little children I fed at Black Panther HQ – and myself in a small way – were what the future was about.

Senator Gene McCarthy of Minnesota, a grey-haired, donnish type, was running for President against the Democratic Party's own national Machine, and many of us young people were going to support him.

We were called his 'children's crusade'.

He told us that it was time for a change. The Convention was going to be held in Chicago and we were determined to help make that change.

Downtown, the streets were filled with newspaper stands, huge walls of print. I read everything, devouring everything.

It was going to be hard, but I was determined to get a college degree. No one on my dad's side of the family had ever done that.

My dad had only gone to primary school. He had to get out as soon as possible to work in the fields back in Mississippi.

Our mother had had to work too. She had lost her father early, and being the eldest of five, had to help.

I was going to get that degree, but the times were exciting, and the papers then were full of Renault Robinson's fight. And the man who joined him, who fought with him, was a state legislator called Harold Washington, the future first black mayor of Chicago.

The Vietnam War was raging on the nightly news each evening, and in our community, on the South Side, we knew that the black men were at war too.

On a cold winter's day, early on a morning at the beginning of December, 1969, Fred Hampton, leader of the Chicago Black Panther Party and creator of 'Breakfast For Children' was shot dead in his sleep by the CPD, while 'resisting arrest'.

The raid involved a white policeman who then went on to advocate and attempt to create a kind of military occupation of the black community. Washington, Robinson and others fought this and won, but there was not a shred of doubt in any of our minds that the police had executed Fred Hampton.

I will never forget the photos of the blood-soaked sheet they had wrapped his body in; or the face of his heavily pregnant girlfriend who had been sleeping beside him. I wonder sometimes what became of her and the child she was carrying.

This was a visceral, life-changing event for everyone my age. Death was all around us, and death had come to claim us: in Vietnam, on the streets of Chicago. We were not children anymore.

University became to me a place in which I would find a direction, a way to make sure that Fred had not died in vain.

I'm still looking.

I returned to feeding the children at the breakfast programme.

We all really did try to keep up appearances for their sake.

But these children knew more about death than most of us middle class people as far as they were concerned could ever imagine. Many of them had lost family members to violence. Fred's death was sad and they would definitely miss his corny jokes, but his demise was just another in their lives and anyway they had come to us to be fed.

Just in that cut-to-the-chase way that a child can drag you back into life when you're not sure that you want to stay in it, we all got back to dishing out the grits and bacon, and milk and eggs and toast that the children needed.

They happily ate, but, we their servers had been altered forever.

(Come to think of it, I wonder if Curtis Mayfield's *Freddy's Dead* on his *Superfly* album is some sort of coded homage to Hampton?)

Sometimes the thoughts that went through my head frightened even me.

A year after Fred's assassination, The 'Five Stairsteps' released a song called *Ooh Child*. *Ooh Child* was to be the pinnacle of their success as a group, but we all thought that it was just the beginning.

The Jacksons were nipping at their heels, but we Chicagoans were going to beat Gary, Indiana.

We all sang the words in that lovely childlike, yearning voice of the lead singer. We all sang the lines that began the song. We had to sing them. They healed us:

'Ooh child, things are gonna get easier.

Ooh, child, they're gonna get brighter

Someday, we'll get it together...'

Pride and Joy

There were three groups of people our parents told us never to answer the door to.

First the Avon Ladies.

The Avon Ladies were usually an unremittingly cheery sort, with lashings of make-up on, bright clothing, and a box full of face paint and potions.

My sister and I loved them. They were like fairy queens, emissaries from another world. Their smell was what you would imagine plastic roses would smell like if plastic roses could smell.

Never taking no for an answer, they would sit on our mother's heavily-plastic-covered couch and proceed, like an old family friend, to display their wares.

What I recall vividly was how quickly they spoke, torrents of words, all about the wonders of their product and how it could change your life.

When I was very small, I would station myself in the midst of an adult conversation, sticking my face up to the speaking adult, just so that I wouldn't miss anything. Adults intrigued me.

Our poor mother spent half her time shooing me away. I was too young, she would declare, to listen to most of the conversations in which she was engaged.

But somehow, the Avon Lady was ok, until mama told her that she had neither the time nor the money to enter the fantasy world the sales lady laid before her, trapped in the jars and bottles of her merchandise.

The next group to avoid were the Jehovah's Witness people.

They were and are completely harmless folk, usually travelling in teams of two, timidly approaching the doors of the houses on Ruby Avenue, knocking quietly and politely, asking to come in and talk.

Somehow my mother always had a sixth sense that they were in the neighbourhood because, at some inner signal, she would break off what she was doing and send us to the windows to draw the curtains.

Our house was what you might call Roman Catholic/Baptist, a collage of practices and beliefs from both churches. What we were not, were Witnesses.

If they ever managed to get inside through some slip in our vigilance, they modestly crept in, their demeanour humble and quiet.

The male Witnesses were sharply dressed and alert, talkative and jolly. The women in those days were drab with a cowed air, and a meek smile, quiet talkers but insistent. What I loved about them all was their sense of mission. How else to explain their insistence on visiting the convent and rectory in the grounds of my primary school in an effort to convert our nuns and priests.

The ones who did that had to be the bravest, the most sure that they were spreading the True Word.

If our mother was bored with her usual routine, she would sit with them for a little while, patiently listening to what they had to say, and afterwards she would inform them that we were Catholic and that was that.

They would sigh and then leave behind a copy of their magazine *The Watchtower*, which I really adored.

Heaven in the pages of *The Watchtower* was like a Disney movie: bright Technicolour vistas stretching towards the horizon; blue, blue cloudless skies, and a world without end.

If their heaven was like that, I'd ask myself, why weren't the women more happy? Paradise looked like a wonderful place.

But the Number one persona non grata was the precinct captain.

A precinct in the United Kingdom can be an architectural or planning term referring to a pedestrianised area.

In America, particularly in Chicago, it means much, much more.

The term is from Medieval Latin and in my old Collins its says: 'precinct: from praecinctum (something) surrounded; from Latin praecingere – to gird around; from 'prae' – before, around + singere (to gird)', a very apt description of what a precinct was on the South Side.

The precinct is technically a minor civil division, part of a county or township, an area which exists for the purpose of conducting elections.

Each precinct has a specific area to which the citizens go to vote and the precinct captain has a roster of addresses. His/her job is to get out the vote.

As the far South Side became more populated with black families, the precinct captains changed from white to black.

They were usually men who came around once in a while to check up on you and make sure that everything was 'ok'.

Back then, in the early days, when you weren't sure that you wouldn't wake up to the sound of bullets piercing your front windows thanks to some local joy-riding good ole' boys, the precinct captain made sure that the local police knew who you were, etc.

He was one of the people, a man with his roots in the Deep South, maybe even a family member.

Precinct captains seemed to go to loads of political meetings on Thursday nights. Dad couldn't go because he worked at night, but when they had the odd one at a time when he could, he was there.

He liked to keep track of these men, guys he would sometimes refer to as 'Uncle Toms', the most dreaded epithet a black person could hurl at another.

Precinct captains in our neighbourhood were always Democrats, always part of 'The Machine', the first Mayor Daley's formidable political operation which had delivered the state to John F. Kennedy a few years earlier, delivered it to his successor Lyndon Baines Johnson, and could do just about anything it wished.

The Democrats were beginning to change from the party of southern oppression and racism, the dreaded 'Dixiecrats' who opposed any move toward black equality, to the party of Civil Rights, of King and Kennedy.

The Chicago black precinct captain was part of all that.

In return he obtained connections. He would become friends with the Ward boss who could refer him up higher in the food chain until the buck stopped at the desk of the Mayor himself. Any citizen who could be relied upon then to turn out and vote for the Dems could be awarded a variety of perks.

No food at Thanksgiving? The precinct captain could turn up with a huge turkey, wrapped in aluminium foil and ready to roast.

Can't play Santa at Christmas? The precinct captain would come by with a not-too-discrete envelope and Christmas would arrive.

It was necessary to insure that the local people continued to vote 'The Machine' in. Playing 'Father Bountiful' was the least that the precinct captain could do.

And he was always 'mine host', whether you were at his house or not.

For the Annual Block Party one summer, our elders dressed up as 'Africans'.

To us at that time, Africa was a romantic place, with one main country, the only one that we wanted to deal with: Egypt.

The other places where someplace else, where our ancestors were transported from. We had no concept of Ghana, Nigeria, Liberia, Senegal, Benin, any of the nations bordering the Atlantic.

We just saw folks who looked dignified one minute, and were running in the streets the next.

Egypt had great stories and the clothes were fabulous but the precinct captain had not bothered to dress up at all.

He arrived in a white, short-sleeved shirt, his belly hanging over his belt.

We kids were never allowed to be present at the parties, so we'd watch from our bedrooms or the kitchen, laughing our heads off at our elders' embarrassing shenanigans.

The funeral director, Mr. Thompson, came dressed as Tutankhamen, a high ball glass in his hand, pretending to be Marvin Gaye.

How Tutankhamen and Marvin Gaye came to be mixed up in one another, I'm not sure, but soon after he arrived, a fight broke out between him and the precinct captain.

They tumbled into Mrs. Smith's carefully trimmed hedge, a hedge that poor old Mr. Smith was constantly being badgered to keep tidy. It collapsed beneath the weight of the pharaoh and the precinct captain, and because we were meant to be otherwise occupied, we couldn't come out and cheer the whole thing on.

Mr. Thompson had called the precinct captain a name, something to do with a promise that had not been fulfilled.

We could hear Mr. Thompson yelling at the top of his voice that Chicago politics could not exist without people like him, people willing to vote 'The Machine' in every time.

Somebody mercifully put on the real Marvin Gaye singing *Pride And Joy* and soon everybody was doing the twist and the entire thing faded into the night.

It was my introduction to 'The Machine' and not the last time I would see its effect on people who had no choice in the matter.

This was part of the tumultuous world of black South Side politics that still existed almost twenty years later when Barack Obama made his decision to return to Chicago after Harvard.

He would have his work cut out for him.

The Broken Boy

In a recent survey taken among black American women, it was reported that many of them had voted for Obama because he was married to Michelle.

They said that Michelle looked like them, had the same body, the same dark skin.

She resembled their sisters, their friends, and they love that Obama – who could have had his pick of anyone – had chosen someone like them.

Someone they could relate to, talk to, a 'sistuh'.

Michelle was 'the change' that they needed.

Before Yardley Cosmetics came to the South Side I used what my mother used. Or tried to.

She's lighter skinned than I am, and one evening, after a typical teenage temper tantrum, I shouted that I was glad that I wasn't as light as she was.

'Black Is Beautiful' was becoming the vogue and my mother with her light coloured hair and skin did not fit the bill. That was fine by me because – at last – I could escape what I thought at the time were her domineering ways.

Ever since we had moved south, she had set down a myriad of

social restrictions, as if we had moved to the grounds of Buckingham Palace. No longer could we do what we considered harmless things like yell at a friend from the other end of the street, or sit on the front step playing music.

She and dad had worked too hard for the house and they wanted to keep it 'respectable'. I just thought that she was being bourgeois, and wanting too much to be admitted to the local Ladies' Society or something like that.

Whenever she was out of the house – on those rare moments when she could spare some seconds for herself – I raided her beauty chest.

I didn't know what in the world she was doing with so many lipsticks and eye brow pencils and foundations anyway. She never had time to go anywhere. But I suppose that didn't stop her from dreaming of her party days before she became pregnant with me and left behind her post-war freedom to embrace the world of 'Betty Crocker' and that ghastly weekend sitcom *Father Knows Best*.

Her lipsticks were bright red which I tried on my lips and cheeks, smiling at myself in her mirroring, trying to see if I could make myself look older. (How strange that there is a point where cosmetics cease to make you older and start to make you look younger!)

Our neighbour on the south side of the house was a kind of Lauren Bacall figure called Mrs. Farrell.

I had learned a lot about Bacall from watching *Saturday Night At The Movies* and she was the slickest woman I could think of.

Like Bacall, Mrs. Farrell moved with a feline elegance and always seemed to be dresses in satin cocktail dressed with slim skirts. She was a bit older than my mother and quite clearly her Dark Side – by that I mean the inner vamp and Woman Of The

World that she had kicked to the kerb when she became a wife and mother.

I could never figure out how Mrs. Farrell wound up in a bungalow in our sleepy South Side community, but I like to think that she was 'saved' by her rather dreary husband, a laconic with an acetic air and the visage of a black Plantagenet.

Of course I bestowed on Mrs. Farrell all sorts of attributes that actually belonged to my fictional Bacall.

Watching her from my tiny sanctuary in the corner of the bedroom that my sisters and I fought over, I could see her in summers stretched out on her chaise lounge under an umbrella. Her long, thin dark legs shone with some sort of oil, and well…she looked like one of those models… like something sleek straight out of the television series *Mad Men*.

Being too short I could never have her grace, and lacking self-confidence, I would never shape the world into accepting me on my terms.

Jackie and I shared these traits, which is the reason we were best friends. We'd both get whistles from white guys speeding past on Halsted, but Jackie hated them and would give them the finger. I just stood looking stupid, intrigued by The Other.

There were times that I would steal Mamma's make-up and go across to Jackie's. Her house was empty because her mother worked.

We'd stand there putting on our mother's base, but it just wouldn't do.

Then one sunny day we came across Yardley Cosmetics and the wonderful world of Jean Shrimpton.

Let me get something straight here: we, little black teen girls from the South Side of Chicago, had no concept of OVERSEAS. Therefore we had no idea what London was about except that the

Queen of England lived there and more importantly, so did Jean Shrimpton.

'The Shrimp' was unbelievably cool. She wore tiny skirts which we attempted one day to the horror of my mother and her best 'you're-not-going-out-looking-like-that!' scream. Shrimpton was beautiful but not impossibly so. We knew girls who could look like Shrimpton with a bit of help. WE could look like Shrimpton with a bit of help...Yardley!

That could only be found at the shopping mall – Evergreen Plaza – deep in 'no-black folks-land'.

In every city in every country on earth, the railroad tracks are the natural demarcation, the natural boundary between peoples and sometimes things. The Illinois Central that I would wake up to in the morning, its lonely whistle calling me to adventure, was the same train whose tracks we dare not cross.

There were stories that the Klan lay in wait on the other side. Black guys in fast cars would venture across and drive deep into the white stronghold known as Beverley Hills, but they came back just as fast.

Jackie and I were, nonetheless, willing to risk the valley of the shadow of death in order to get our hands on 'The Shrimp's' mascara and lipstick.

The bus going west on 95th Street deposited all of the black people it contained at our corner. No people of colour got on. Except us, one Saturday in spring.

We sat in the back, almost holding hands.

As the good citizens of Beverley Hills climbed on, they eye-balled us hard, but we held steadfast. All we had to do was pick up some make-up and get back to where we lived. We wanted to tell them that we had no intention of moving into their 'hood.

The ride to that shopping mall was one of the longest rides on any bus that I've ever taken. A gang of white guys got on and we conjured up images of some local 'Bubba' ringing round to his mates to tell them that there're some 'niggra gals' on the bus.

We knew the stories. Everyone knew them. We grew up with the stories of black women kidnapped and gang-raped while walking down the street, or going to school or to church.

We grew up knowing the story of Emmet Till – our South Side martyr, who had gone down to Mississippi to visit relatives in the mid '50's, and had would up dead in the Pearl River.

Chicago's black paper, *The Defender*, a champion against lynching and for black equality ever since its founding at the beginning of the century, started a campaign to keep young Emmett's name and what happened to him alive.

Emmett Till was a 14 year old black boy from Chicago who was murdered in 1955 in Money Mississippi, near where our father was born, a small unincorporated town near Greenwood which lies on the Tallahatchie River.

He had been there visiting relatives and being a Chicagoan, more than likely ignored the local etiquette.

Accounts differ, but he may have whistled at a white woman, on a dare from his young friends.

Whatever happened, two of the locals decided to 'teach the boy' a lesson.

He was kidnapped after midnight from the house he was staying in, driven to a shed on a plantation in a county called Sunflower, beaten to a pulp, shot dead, a 70-pound cotton gin fan tied to his neck with barbed wire, and finally his weighed down body was dropped in the Tallahatchie.

The heads of the black Civil Rights organization, the NAACP, disguised themselves as sharecroppers and set out to find the missing boy. No wonder Nina Simone sang: *Mississippi Godamn*.

We all grew up knowing Emmett's story, knowing about the viewing of his decomposed body in the open coffin at his funeral at the fierce insistence of his mother, her beauty destroyed forever.

The all-white jury took 67 minutes and said that it would have taken shorter time if they hadn't stopped off to cool their thirst with a soda.

America and Europe exploded, and the murder of Emmett Till is known as the hate crime that changed America.

There is a school named after him on the South Side, the only school so far in Chicago named after a child.

A play has been written about an imaginary meeting between Emmett and Ann Frank, two children whose destiny was to meet murder and in their death be given immortality.

Baldwin, Toni Morrison, and Langston Hughes amongst others have created writings on the subject and Bob Dylan released a song about Emmett Till in '62, the year Jackie and I sat trembling on that bus as we went in search of the perfect pink lipstick.

It turned out that the boys were more interested in discussing the White Sox than us, though that didn't stop us from imagining Klan hoods on their heads.

Needless to say that we where treated as if we had just dropped down from Mars – no, worse, Martians would have been paid attention to.

We were ignored until crazy Jackie started wondering aloud why we weren't being served. Someone suddenly showed up after everybody turned around and we bought a lipstick each and some mascara. The make-up was too light.

The ride back was without incident, and, as Jackie played her Supremes disc before her parents came home from work, we pretended to be Shrimpton.

Our alternative was the stunning Cicely Tyson, who we saw on tv, who wore her hair closed cropped and natural.

The two images stood in our young minds: Tyson and Shrimpton, and then, a few years later, Twiggy, who we had no qualms in trying to imitate, except that Jackie grew more voluptuous and eventually she couldn't be bothered with anything but her job and the nightclubs of the South Side.

The Flood

Jerry Butler, Commissioner for the 8th district of Cook County, the county that Chicago is in, is a man who writes policy for his constituents by day, dealing happily with the minutiae of everyday life, and by nights still gives concerts as the magnificent solo soul act that he still is.

I mean, can any other town boast a politician on the local level who used to be part of an epoch making group – The Impressions, who was once known as 'The Ice Man', and could hold his own on a stage with that 'Beautiful Brother', Curtis Mayfield?

Senator Barack Obama rushes to the telephone in his Senate office.

Through the help of his staff he has just scored a major victory in a hearing on a particular piece of legislation. He has also attained an alliance with a powerful Senator and so he is calling his wife back in Chicago to tell her the good news.

Michelle has refused to uproot herself and her daughters and move to Washington. She's staying on the South Side.

She listens. She replies by telling him that there are ants in the kitchen. And in the upstairs bathroom. Could he buy a few ant traps on his way back to Chicago the following night? She had to pick up their daughters and before that, attend a meeting. In other words, real life beckoned.

Obama agrees, hangs up the telephone and wonders if any other Senator, after having achieved the first stage of an arms proliferation bill, would be greeted at home by a request for the ant version of *Roach Motel* ('they check in, but they don't check out!')

Every spring, the lovingly nurtured basements on our street flooded.

The basement in those days was the recreation room, and also the 'den', the masculine domain of the man in the house.

The den was the mark of how far these sons of sharecroppers and railroad workers had come along the path of the American Dream.

Before that, they had been mere workers, cogs in the machine, anonymous, useful only as pack animals who could answer back.

But on Ruby Avenue, South Side of Chicago, they could create their own spaces, their own lairs.

The part of the basement which housed the den was also a source of competition amongst the fathers on our street. I would say that our father's look was mid sixties or so, the time he had finally amassed enough money to convert it.

Others reflected ideas about hunting lodges in Imperial Russia (stuffed heads, replicas of rifles, some were actual rifles); Hollywood – chrome and white, plush bar stools; some were like a Saul Bass montage in the opening credits of a late Hitchcock film like *Vertigo* – lots of geometric, Mondrian-like shapes in strong pastel colours.

When the men had the time and space from their jobs on various assembly lines, they would gather in one another's dens, drink hard liquor judiciously and listen to their record collections.

Our Dad collected lots of different music, but the man down the street, the ultra-cool Mr. Kendrick, had a DJ brother and so collected all of the soul, the known and the unknown, the famous and the obscure.

He even had some recordings of West Side doo-wop, made somewhere by local groups.

That was a sound that I knew and appreciated.

I had spent my early childhood in an apartment of the building my dad and his sister and husband co-owned on the West Side.

Unlike the tidy bungalow he eventually bought on the South Side, the West Side house was closer to a New York Brownstone in Chelsea. There was a sweeping gate, stairs leading up to the double entrance, two beautifully elaborate doors made in the grand old 'robber baron' days of the 1890's, and a huge garden in the back with some sort of nude Greek-ish statue, painted white atop a defunct water fountain which the birds would walk around in full of despair.

The basement of that house spanned the length of the floor space of the mansion, and I learned to roller skate in it and run through it screaming at the top of my lungs as the damsel in distress to my younger sister's superman.

That basement flooded, too, but delicately. Tiny streams ran down the concrete floor from time to time and we helped our mother furiously clean it up. I was personally pleased that there was no damage to the 'Watteau' wallpaper, a conduit for my daydreams of life in Paris sometime in the future.

Our old West Side house is a crack den now, broken windows, the lovely wrought iron banisters gone, a haunted, dark place that the local children make fun of, and the police ignore.

But Ruby Avenue was not Belle Epoque. It was sturdy and middle class.

When the floods came, the water could be ankle deep, and

needless to say, would ruin everything. Everyone would literally bail one another out.

Once a Big Flood destroyed many of our baby pictures and the photos of my parents' wedding, with me onboard already, my mother's tummy gently rounded beneath her folded hands. By the time that big flood came to our basement, our father had taken on an extra job, repairing televisions.

Somehow, in between working on the assembly line six nights a week, he had taken himself on a course to learn how to fix tv's. I always have to laugh when black people are accused of being lazy.

Black men and women worked hard and still do. To land a man who could literally 'sit you down', make it possible that you did not have to go outside the home to work, was a blessing and the ultimate catch.

Happily the flood had happened before my Father had accumulated other people's boxes in our basement.

Nevertheless, the flood was a blow. The local black plumbers were being rushed off their feet, and the possibility of halting further water damage looked remote.

We could not help in any useful way. The floor needed to be drained.

I think then, since the years of my parents' marriage mirrored my own, their marriage was going through its early adolescent stage, accompanied by a suddenly stroppy, eldest child.

I had grandly announced to my mother the day of the flood that there was no way that I would emulate her life-children, an apron around her waist all of the time, a husband to whom she seemed subservient.

Women were meant to work. To earn their own money. To live.

A few days later, the basement was drained and things were not as bad as we had feared. Photos could be cleaned up, clothes cleaned.

The den had survived intact, and the men soon could resume their bragging and tall tales.

I'm pretty sure that my parents were not speaking to one another the Saturday night the Kendricks' threw their celebration party after the basements' were saved.

As usual, I had to baby-sit, the baby-mad days of my childhood, when my three younger brothers and a sister were born and I was enamoured with the three most beautiful children I had ever seen in my life, were long, long gone.

I could hear the music flooding out of the Kendricks house.

I listened to his collection – soul: the great Betty Everett who crooned: *Just One Look*, one of the greatest renditions of coupe de foudre ever made; Gene Chandler – The immortal 'Duke of Earl' – who rumour had it, was going to get himself a cape and a monocle in the near future in order to truly become the Duke; The Dells, whose falsetto lead Johnny Carter sounded to me like what an archangel must have sounded like; Barbara Lewis with her heartbreakingly seductive *Hello Stranger*.

Mr. Kendrick also managed to have some sides on hand that had been recorded by The Vibrations, who were so 'Inside Baseball' on some levels, that you had to be a real soul aficionado to collect them.

As I sat listening for any sounds of death from my sleeping brothers and sisters upstairs, I made up my mind to hit the road as soon as I was old enough.

I was not going to juggle motherhood, the work I wanted to do in the world, and flooded basements.

I was going to be free.

Life on the South Side meant family, no matter what you

wanted to do.

Family life, its peaceful cycle of routine, had been too hard-won.

I was restless, ambitious to see the world.

I could not reconcile flooded basements with that.

Destination

At some point in time in our small community, there were two destinations of choice: Heaven and Africa.

Heaven had always been a part of our lives, although its intensity and immediacy at the every day level depended on what religion – if any – was practiced.

Heaven for Protestants, which invariably meant Baptists, was a thing shouted for on Sundays, shaken down and sprinkled around with as much force as humanly possible, and then brought to earth.

Heaven was not its own reward, but the pay-back and the reason to live for many.

It was the ultimate. There was nothing else.

After all, life itself had been troublesome enough, full of uncertainty and fear for these sons and daughters of sharecroppers.

Life could be nasty brutish and short, or nasty brutish and long, but one thing was for sure: it was always necessary to have a destination in mind.

Things could happen that were impossible to control and too often those things depended on what could not be controlled: the colour of your skin.

In my own family, for instance, we were many shades.

My mother's father had grey eyes and my mother had frizzy

ash-blonde hair, like the hair seen in the portraits of those doomed aristocratic ladies, painted before the Revolution – their jaunty, huge country bonnets perched rakishly on mounds of thick, coarse, dusky blonde hair.

The life of those portraits, like the faux-Watteau wallpaper on the basement wall of our old place on the West Side, created a destination for me, one in my eye and in my heart.

But there was another, public, destination, one that I could share with my fellow South Siders, that I could show through photos that I had taken, and through those photos, and my tales and bits and pieces, inspire others to go forward. Inspiration being a very important South Side virtue.

Heaven could only be reached by one route in most cases, leaving the other destination the only one possible in this life: Africa.

To be honest, we had no more knowledge of the continent than any other group of Americans, but the citizens of my community prided themselves on thinking that they did.

In their conversations and in the books I was given to read by some of them as I grew up, Africa appeared as nothing more than a country – perhaps the size of the United State – but it was always lush and beautiful and fertile and available.

This Africa was populated with 'Africans', people who looked a bit like us and who were all, without doubt, nobility.

One of my earliest memories in the realm of political affairs was seeing the face of a defeated Patrice Lumumba in the paper.

He was pictured in black and white, as was everything in those days, but I particularly recall is his look of despair, of hopelessness.

I knew nothing about him except that he was African and dead, a state of affairs some of my fellow Chicagoans would have advocated, the ones who rang our telephone at night offering free passage 'back to Africa.'

One of my friends from school, Edlita, and her family were moving to Africa.

Her father was fed up with the struggle to maintain the type of middle-class existence that had become the norm after the war: mom at home, dad out to work.

He had tried several professions – he had a university degree- but met racism at every turn.

A white organization was offering – over a radio station – to send any black people 'back to Africa' who wished to go there.

There were negotiations going on, telephone calls back and forth etc.

But the whole thing turned out to be the attempt by some racist to draw attention to his point of view.

The fact that they were not going to Africa after all, plunged Edlita's father into despair.

He wouldn't talk to anyone. He would just sit on his front porch night and day that summer, until the police took him away.

Edlita and her family had to move soon after. They had lost their house.

Maybe in the end, he did get to Africa.

Maybe that was where he was as he sat on that porch, staring into the distance.

By the middle of the sixties more shop fronts around our house opened selling African and faux-African wares.

These places were invariably run by someone with a long, unpronounceable name that you'd suspiciously think might be something cobbled together from various inauthentic sources.

You entered either an atmosphere of gloom or doom, greeted very solemnly by the 'brother' and/or 'sister' who ran the place,

I can say practically without exception that those shop owners with their righteous ways were a pretty Calvinistic lot, almost Stalinist in their interpretation of Africa and all things African.

Never mind that they had never been to the continent themselves and couldn't see themselves going there in the near future. That small detail did not stop them – without shame – idling an entire afternoon away talking about a place they'd only visited in books.

Some of which were highly dubious. Ludicrous even, which I put down to a quality which was not African, but very American: the disbelief in the Official Version.

This is how that notion works:

You are told one thing. But of course, you don't believe it because it is The Official Version of events or the life of a person.

On the South Side, in the case of black people, the Official Version was never believed.

This disbelief would be stated somewhere in the title, or implied. And that disbelief the majority of the time consisted of this: there were more black people, more people who were black and never acknowledged to be black than we know.

The wife of George the Third had African blood. Charlotte was a Mecklenberg-Strelitz and they were known for that. (Hmm, the Queen's lips did look unusually full when she was younger…)

Cleopatra was black.

Ok, I know that she was descended from a Macedonian general, but as one of those books asked: who was her mother?

Beethoven was black. Abraham Lincoln. Napoleon. Everybody was black in fact. So you walked around with this assuredness that the world and history had got it all very badly wrong.

Of course you dare not challenge the bookshop people. To do that wasn't worth it because they lived for long, complex, and convoluted argumentation, usually with the index pointing up or at you as they spoke.

Once – and only once – did I ask what difference it made if these eminent people had been black? If they were, so what? Beethoven hadn't done anything to alleviate slavery, plus he backed the guy who started it up again, Napoleon.

Governor Shalid, formerly James Frenelle, who owned 'Afro Books, Gifts And Incense' would love it when I came in.

James and I had grown up in the same community, but had become estranged due to the nature of his conversion to extreme blackness.

The effect of this conversion was devastating.

First of all the conversion brought about the end of his relationship with his stepfather.

His stepfather had been a first generation Pole born in Detroit. James' natural father had been shot dead on the West Side.

The simple fact that he would go often to the West Side – that Hades as far as we were concerned – to gamble signalled the real possibility of his eventual doom, and thus it had come to pass.

The circumstances of James' mother's marriage to his stepfather are clouded in mystery, but there was no doubt in anyone's mind that the Polish man was in love.

As a consequence of his decision to marry a black woman he had been cut off from his family completely. Rumour had it that the man's mother would only consider admitting him back into the fold if he would go and see a psychiatrist.

If you looked through the window, it was possible to see James' dad at the lounge on the corner of Halsted Street, a fixture in the community.

He was also an ardent Gladys Knight and the Pips fan, blasting their music on Saturday mornings in summer. And if Smokey Robinson had ever walked through his door, he would have died and gone to heaven

He had adopted this hip tone to his voice which gave his twangy Detroit vowels a kind of Southern slur which some people in the neighbourhood took as homage and others took as offence.

James, as he became black, had become one of the latter.

It was tragic. The man truly loved his stepfather, who had given him everything, but the purity of his beliefs would not allow him to see through his fundamentalism to the truth.

He and my best friend Jackie dated briefly after highschool, but James had become much too fanatical for anyone to see him seriously as date material.

She finally hit the nightclubs – and her fate – leaving James to his 'black' Bible, his 'black' Koran, his 'black' Torah.

This staying with one's own, this cherishing one's own, has always been a part of the South Side.

And sometimes it could become pathological.

Don't Get Lost

Barack Obama has come to Kenya, a man on the run.

Before that, he has travelled in Europe, walked through town square, ridden on a bus with a man from Senegal who offered him his meagre water at the end of their ride.

In Kenya he is greeted by his half-sister, and shortly after, by his auntie.

They proceed to visit the rest of his extended family, the family that his dead father – 'The Old Man' – had made.

He is half of this land, half of the women driving him to the family compound.

His auntie is dropped off and says to Barack: "Don't get lost."

Obama is not sure what that means.

Some people forget to write. Some people never come back.

It came as a shock to Michelle Obama, at Princeton, to face the fact that the higher she went up the ladder, the less likely it would be that she would stay close to her community.

In her undergrad thesis she wrote about this estrangement.

Why could she not take a kind of South Side value system with her through life rather than leave it behind?

She could not have known that her leaving, that leaving behind of all that is known, is also the foundation of her return.

A friend came to visit me in London my first six months here.

He had had a destination in mind: a city that played The Beatles around the clock. Never mind that this was the late '80's, Eric thought it was true.

We found together a record shop that sold vintage records.

Then we spent the night in his cramped, cheap hotel room near the British Museum, listening to all of the Four Tops' records we had bought, Levi Stubbs' heart-breaking tenor blasting from his boom box, blasting out home to both of us.

In the end, no matter what he had said or done, home was Eric's ultimate destination.

The expat knows this. Exile, expatriation, in time, demonstrates that there is, indeed, a destination, this other country, one that neither resembles the one settled in, nor the one left behind.

Even if exile, expatriation is only a few miles from where you were born.

Michelle Obama began to work in the Loop after returning to Chicago.

She has stated that she remembers looking out of the window of her downtown office, unable to see the South Side that she knew and loved.

She had left it behind. Or so she feared.

She had gone to another place, another country.

That one was much harder to return from.

It was 1988 and she took a job at the law firm where she would meet Barack Obama. It was a corporate law firm and this was the time for a brilliant, Ivy-League educated back woman lawyer to make her mark in the legal world.

This is everything that her parents had hoped for, this destination, a major job placement, and she had worked so hard, endured so much, her graduate and post graduate life had been for this.

Then her beloved father dies from the complications of surgery and a close friend dies, too, after this, causing her to ponder the meaning of her life.

This is when, she has said, she made the decision to bring her skills to the community that made her, go back, and retrace her steps, re-enter the country of her birth, her destination.

She is following a pattern.

Soon after the First World War, black people began travelling, moving around, searching.

The idea of staying in one place, of being confined to one place had become both a curse and a desire.

The notion of home, that place that could belong to you without fear, and in comfort was what they longed for.

In the past, heaven was the only place that could define this home.

In my generation, there was the search for Africa and we would hand that desire and that search, that destination, down.

For me, being there caused Africa to lose its amorphous, America-romantic essence.

It narrowed itself down to the tumultuous airport of Accra, and became smaller still, as I climbed the ramparts of Elmina Castle where the enslaved had been held before they were forced on boats for the voyage into the void. I stood and looked out over the black Atlantic and felt a kind of exhilaration that someone in my bloodline had decided to live.

At Elmina, at this destination, our South Side myths dissolved into the reality of crumbling architecture, children begging on the road and posh hotels where the water stopped at night and people lived on the other side of a barbed wire fence.

I had to smile when I watched on tv the First Lady of the United States fussing with her daughter's topknot as they made their way through the ramparts of Cape Castle, another slave fort.

There had been rumours all over the news that she was to be made Queen Of Cape Coast in honour of her ancestor, Jim Robinson, who know doubt had set sail in chains from that very coastline.

Her mother and another lady are walking behind, dressed in simple trousers and loose blouses that any mother would wear on a shopping expedition to the local shopping mall in Hyde Park.

Michelle has that weary walk, her belly slightly forwards, her lower back slightly arched.

I've seen that walk so many times on the streets of the community I was born in.

I see Michelle Obama walking through that castle of shame and despair with her mother and her daughters.

And I smile again.

She has stopped Sasha, to tend to her hair, twisting the topknot and making it just so.

Sasha is the first person born in the 21st Century to live in the White House.

Michelle pats Sasha's hair in place.

They continue.

This woman, her family, I know them.

Wall Of Sound

It didn't surprise me one bit that the first prize that President Obama awarded in the White House was to Stevie Wonder.

He and the First Lady presented him with The Gershwin Prize For Popular Song.

It think it was also a 'thank you' for being a big part of the sound of their coming together. He was one of the composers of their 'Obamamusic'

Signed, Sealed, Delivered and *I Was Born To Love Her* formed the backdrop to my teen years.

It was about the boys me and my friends wished were in our lives.

We'd look at the models in *Ebony*, a national black magazine published in Chicago. We drooled over the slick, manly models, particularly Richard Roundtree who went on to play *Shaft* a decade later.

Sidney Poitier was our special idol and to us, the most beautiful man in the world. Well, he and Paul Newman tied in that position.

I was chaperoned on dates by my younger brother until I was eighteen. If I didn't like it, I stayed sitting in my window looking out. Our mothers had been taught to be prim and proper because, as a black woman, any deviation from that left you open to being accused of loose living or much worse.

I had various 'boyfriends', guys from my school who had to sit with my dad and be vetted as I sat on the other side of the room squirming, the plastic cover that kept our couch clean squealing noisily.

My first sneak out of the house was to see James Brown and his Famous Flames at the Regal Theatre.

My little brother – after a suitable bribe – was meant to provide an alibi for me. The alibi was that I was out with Lucius.

Jackie and I found our seats near the front and waited for the show to begin.

Then I saw Lucius with the 'fastest' girl in our school, the one who ragged me when I first joined. I couldn't believe it!

First up were The Flames, featuring the magnificent Maceo Woods on sax. The band played for an hour. It was amazing, and then suddenly, in the wings, we heard the cry of 'Please, please, please, please'…and on walked James Brown, his face already covered in sweat, pleading to his imaginary girlfriend not to leave him.

The only time I have since seen that level of intensity onstage was when a drag queen in Nice decades later sang Brel's *Ne me quite pas* – 'Don't Leave Me' – with sweat pouring down her face.

I was torn between watching arguably the greatest black star on the planet give two hours of his all, and watching Lucius kissing my enemy.

Let me be clear: at that point Lucius was tainted goods, but I couldn't let HER get away with this. I knew somehow that this was about me, not him.

That was the beginning of a week of shocks.

The next happened while listening to our local superstar DJ Herb Kent, 'The Kool Gent'.

While in the middle of washing dishes, I suddenly heard a strange sound coming from a show that was practically nothing but wall-to-wall Motown: Cicero Blake with his smooth croon; Gene Chandler, part doo-wop, part pop; the silky Chi-lites; the masculine baritone of Tyrone Davis; the epic Etta James and the fantastic Vibrations, to name just a few.

These people and this sound was my afternoon, after school, washing dishes in the kitchen or doing my homework.

Then suddenly, this strange, plinky guitar intro came on and the voice of ...Paul McCartney! My soul station was playing The Beatles!

Of course The Beatles had made a mark on the South Side. They had been in and out of the States for a few years and had even appeared in Chicago, but none of us ventured out to see them. Only the most avant-garde South Sider would have been in the audience.

I had to stop what I was doing as I tried to imagine what a 'paperback rider' was. I just couldn't get my head around it.

At the end of this explosion, Lucius rang to explain himself. I took the phone into the bathroom so that I could hear above the normal din of our house.

Interestingly, Lucius always managed to ring me up to apologize at epoch making moments. The last time before we broke up was the evening of the assassination of Martin Luther King. I sat on the closed toilet, listening to his rubbish, Lucius not knowing what had just happened. I stopped him and told him, and we both burst into tears.

In the neighbouring state of Indiana, at the same time, Bobby Kennedy was telling a black audience the terrible news during one of his campaign rallies for President. Kennedy was himself assassinated a few weeks later.

Indianapolis descended into shock and mourning. The South Side and the rest of Chicago exploded.

But that was a few years in the future.

Right now I was dealing with a revolution.

As I finished my work and sat down to watch the local dance show *Soul Train*, the black version of the national dance show *The Dick Clark Show*, I think that I knew that something had shifted.

With all that was going on: the move away from the word 'Negro' and 'coloured' into 'black'; the fact that we young people were beginning to question the relatively comfortable existence we lived – in comparison to black people who lived in the housing estates, and the tenements that Dr. King had tried to destroy. My preoccupations were slowly starting to look trivial and I wondered what way things were going to go.

Jackie Wilson appeared on television later that night singing *Lonely Teardrops*, surrounded by shimmying girls.

My mother remarked that they were not wearing enough clothes, but I saw a genius, a man who could dance beautifully and sell a song like no one else.

When Jackie had that heart attack onstage in the mid-'70's, singing the last line from *Lonely Teardrops*, falling over, hitting his head and going into a vegetative state, Elvis showed up and paid all of his medical bills until the day he died.

Some folks knew this about Elvis and he gained a respect in the community that he had never really had.

A few years after that first night that I saw Jackie, a little boy appeared, the newest member of The Jacksons. Michael was tiny, with an uncanny ability to make you believe that he knew what he was saying when he sang those big love songs…and he danced like Jackie Wilson. Part of Michael's appeal to me was that he channelled Jackie. They had the same quality.

The 'Kool Gent' had set off a war inside of me: Motown and Chi-town versus Phil Spector's *Wall Of Sound* and The Beatles.

I veered between them, not sure where I belonged, not sure where I wanted to go.

The South Side was about the former and I knew that somewhere inside me, I was moving toward the later, or at least a synthesis of the two sounds.

Martin Luther King, a year before my hearing *Paperback Writer* for the first time, had refused to cross the bridge at Selma, Alabama during a civil rights march, changing the direction, too, of the Movement itself.

He had been issued with a restraining order… and he had obeyed it.

We young people, witnessing this, turned, too.

It was clear that Dr. King no longer spoke for us, turning the other cheek no longer spoke to us.

Unknown to me, I was going in another direction in more than one sense.

I decided then that it was better to lie and sneak out and date who I wanted than to be subjected to the rigid vetting my parents insisted upon.

I was heading toward Spector and The Beatles.

Higher And Higher

Chicago. Summer of '09.

Sitting in a soul food restaurant a few streets from the Obama family home, I notice that there's jerk chicken on the menu.

The waitress tells me that this is a new thing – the combination of Southern 'roadside food', sometimes called 'soul food', and Caribbean cuisine.

Someone in the corner is rhapsodising about Michelle's organic vegetable garden at the White House and the fact that the President often eats his vegetarian meals in a specially prepared box featuring the vegetables. And that he can cook Indonesian dhal, too.

I remember Jackie calling me across the street on Ruby Avenue to see a new cookbook she had purchased called *Vibration Cooking,* by the greatest writer I had ever read, Vertamae Grosvenor.

The book was a combination memoir-travelogue, and a listing of her favourite recipes, soul food all.

We read them avidly and Jackie even tried a few.

We sat back listening to Dusty Springfield who was wondrous and miraculous to us with her warm, silvery voice, and Shirley Bassey who was the most extraordinary black woman we had ever seen come out of Britain.

Dusty in particular confounded us, made us look again at our rigid definitions, just as Vertamae made us see the food that we had eaten all of our lives as rich and strange.

We had to question everything. And we tried.

What's the difference between rhythm and blues and soul?

Ask the music industry because they invented the terms.

The term 'rock and roll' was invented in the late '40's to describe what was called 'urbane, rocking, jazz-based music with a heavy, insistent beat' and was beginning to take the race music world by storm.

'Little Richard' put himself in that category, and every other category there was because – and he was right – he WAS r'n'b and soul and gospel, too.

So I guess that you have to listen and see if you can hear the difference yourself. Experts say that they can. So I guess so.

In 1960, our baby sister was born, soon after we moved to our red brick bungalow on Ruby Avenue. Penny is the only child in our family to have never lived anywhere except the South Side.

At the time of her birth, our mother, who was one month short of her thirty-third birthday, and our father, who had just turned thirty-six two weeks before, had borne a total of seven children.

Seven egos, plus their own, in a tiny house my father worked night and day for, had to produce stress levels that I cannot possibly imagine.

To blow it off, they sometimes went to the basement, put on Louis Jordan and danced.

Louis Jordan was the subject of the show *Five Guys Named Moe*. I can remember his songs because we used to sing them jumping around the kitchen table: *Caledonia* – 'Caledonia, Caledonia, what makes your big head so hard!'

We all sang songs as soon as we could talk properly and that's no exaggeration.

Babies and little kids loved his music because it was silly and full of life.

It was called 'jump' – that antecedent of r'n'b and soul. And jump is what it made us do: *Ain't Nobody Here But Us Chickens*; *Salt Pork, West Virginia; Let The Good Times Roll*; dad's favourite: *Beware, Brother, Beware*; *Stone Cold Dead in the Market*; the rumba and cha-cha of *Run Joe* and *Open The Door Richard*. Our middle sister Regina, born with the same ash blonde fuzzy hair as our mother and thus called 'Chicken Little' by dad, used to croon in her baby voice: 'I ain't got nothin' but the blooos…'

We were 'Choo Choo Ch'Boogie... take me right back to the shack…Jack!'

That was Louis Jordan.

Sam Cooke came along, first in gospel, and then became a 'traitor' to the form and crossed over and made *Chain Gang*, which is considered, by those who know, as r'n'b, as well as Chubby Checkers' *The Twist* which I would call pop, but there you go.

Chicago soul is a style of soul music that some would say has a rich Southern flavour, loads of gospel, soft, a bit of orchestration here and there, laid-back

By the way, 'house' – which evolved in a highly electronic way out of soul – originated in Chicago, some say at the club Warehouse, a gay club where Frankie Nichols used to mix and which I frequented in the mid-'70's before moving to NYC and the Garage which had roughly the same scene and the same sound.

Chicago soul is and was: Jerry Butler; Cicero Blake; Fontella Bass; The Artistics; Gene Chandler; The Chi-Lites; Tyrone Davis;

Betty Everett; The Impressions; Etta James; The Vibrations and Jackie Wilson.

After JFK, Sam Cooke was the first person in my young life who had meant a lot to me and was shot and killed.

Growing up on the South Side of Chicago, he wasn't to be the last.

At the beginning of 1964, a few months after the assassination of JFK, Sam Cooke recorded *A Change Is Gonna Come*, an answer to Bob Dylan's song *Blowin' In The Wind* – a song which Cooke himself covered and which he said he could never have imagined a white guy having enough of an understanding of oppression to ever create.

His song *A Change Is Gonna Come* is immortal, played at the funeral of Malcolm X and invoked by Obama in Chicago the night that he had become the 44th President Of the United States: 'It's been a long time coming, but tonight, because of what we did on this day, in this election, at this defining moment, change has come to America.'

It had indeed, but lovely and appropriate as Sam's song was, I think that a more Chicago tune, a more apt sentiment that night beside the Lake would have been the exuberant, fate-defying soul anthem of Jackie Wilson: *Higher And Higher*.

JAZZ

Prepare To Do Something Else

OS vs. NS

Obama's first foray into politics was the Democratic primary race for the Illinois General Assembly in the mid '90's.

Wisely, he decided to go for a safe seat.

He wanted to become a state senator.

Since the Republican Party is practically non-existent on the South Side, whoever won the nomination won the seat.

How he wound up being the sole name on the primary ballot and therefore Illinois senator de facto is mired in controversy.

It would not be fair to unpick that controversy here without all relevant parties having a say, but it is clear that class played its ugly part in it.

Obama is a graduate of the ultra-elite Harvard Law School with the equivalent of a First.

He had been the first black American to head the prestigious *Harvard Law Review*, and as a result, over 600 law firms had enquired about him around the time of his graduation.

By then, Obama had decided to return to Chicago and take up a practice with a law firm which specialized in civil rights legislation, a not unusual state of affairs in America for someone who has an eye on politics.

At the same time, he began *Dreams* and began making himself known on the South Side as a bridge-builder.

He had boldly strode right into the complex web that is the South Side.

That he hadn't paid 'his dues', which some alleged; or made the necessary deference to the lions and lionesses of the community, which others alleged; or just plain didn't wait his turn in relation to older, more rooted politicians, are complaints levelled against him by some South Siders even today.

He was a young man in a hurry and if he got things a bit wrong, well, as the French say '*tant pis* – so what?

Barack Obama had bigger fish to fry.

But Harvard Law, *magna cum laude*; the *Law Review*; Teacher of Constitutional Law at the University of Chicago; these facts made him seem, to some South Siders, to be nothing less than a one-man Third Column; a Trojan Horse for more sinister forces.

The influx to the North, from the rural South, after World War One is called the Great Migration.

It exploded the black population on the South Side that had been there prior to the war: the 'Old Settlers' (OS).

The War had halted Eastern and Southern European immigration, therefore causing industrialists to turn to the Caribbean and to the deep South, imprisoned as it was in harsh anti-black laws: The Black Codes.

In the OS days, the 'Levee' was where the majority of the night clubs on the South Side existed, located close to the heart of the city.

The 'Levee' was named after the area of the same name in New Orleans. The name had arrived with Dixieland, the matrix of all jazz known as 'Chicago Style.'

Inspite of the fact that bohemian whites looking for the buzz crawled all over the area, it was fairly contained.

Harlem was gaining ascendancy, and the title of 'Capital of Black America', partly because of the housing explosion in what was seen to be countryside in New York at the end of the 19th Century, and black people flooding in seeking work as servants and other service workers. In Chicago, the southern migration was from the small pre-war 'Black Belt' further south, creating 'Bronzeville'.

The OS detested the New Settlers largely for two reasons: their southerness; and their youth.

But when the 'Red Summer' of 1919 came, with its ferocious race riots breaking out throughout America, many of the OS blamed these on the NS being...the 'n' word is applicable here.

They blamed the NS for the white people who came into the area in the '30's and '40's looking for illicit fun and the music of Louis Armstrong; the majestic King Oliver at the Savoy Ballroom; and Lil Hardin Armstrong, the wife of 'Satchmo' and a major jazz pianist in her own right.

Satchmo's' second wife, Hardin was a singer, a composer, an arranger and bandleader. Her compositions were considered classics, including *Just For A Thrill* which Ray Charles revived and made into a hit in 1959.

Lil even provided a hit for Ringo Star after her death – *Bad Boy*.

Hardin had moved to Chicago after graduating from Fisk, the eminent black university. There she met Jelly Roll Morton, who, she subsequently wrote, taught her pedal technique and how to attack a keyboard, in an impromptu master class that she would never forget.

After various small jobs and lying to her relatively upper class parents who had OS sensibilities, Lil took a job at Dreamland, the centre of Chicago nightlife.

She played with King Oliver's band there, had a brief marriage to a singer divorced, him, then fell for the young cornet player that King Oliver had imported from New Orleans in order to keep an eye on his competition: one Louis Armstrong.

Lil liked his potential and set about changing him from NS to OS, which better suited his new life in Chicago.

She later married him. He betrayed her, but in later life she became his friend again.

She was always the jazz pianist's jazz pianist, a master in every way. She lived in Chicago at the end, and died at her piano, recording a tribute to Satchmo.

There was the Plantation Café on 35th Street which catered to a white clientele and was closed because of Prohibition violations. The OS accused the NS of being magnets for whites who wanted to walk on the wild side, often in the front gardens and the backyards of the OS.

West Indians seemed to be exempt from this general condemnation because they were seen as conservative and small-business owning.

But at times they fell foul of the Old Settlers, too, sometimes called 'monkey-chasers' by them and worse.

In time, the OS began to check out the clubs to see what was going on and to observe the NS just like the whites did.

Some of the clubs were segregated from top to bottom. Literally.

You might find Bricktop and Florence Mills downstairs, where the mainly white clientele and OS partied, and Alberta Hunter upstairs with the NS.

Jews and Italians could shuttle up and down. They were considered to be somewhere between black and white.

For some of the NS and their descendants (like me), who had in time become the majority, Barack Obama had aspects of OS culture. He pushed (and for some still does) all the wrong buttons.

Club DeLisa

My boyfriend in my last year in highschool was named Randall, his mother was a typical OS.

She let it be known that her ancestors had been freemen, and had had enough money to buy their families out of enslavement.

I suppose that's why she insisted that I always wore gloves in her house.

Randall had green eyes, and was considered to be a great catch.

We even had an entry in our highschool yearbook for the student with 'the prettiest eyes' which always went to the blue-eyed, the green-eyed, and the hazel-eyed.

His mother tolerated me because, I guess, she saw me as her beloved son's 'wild oats' that must be sown. But there was no way that he was taking me to the senior prom. That privilege was reserved for Cecilia, she of the OS tendency, complete with blue-green eyes and pale skin.

Randall asked me over to the family manse in 'Pill Hill' where all of the doctors lived in splendour. When he wimped out and told me that he couldn't take me I couldn't believe that this was happening in the middle of the Black Power Movement, Black solidarity and blah-blah-blah. He gave me the news dressed in a dashiki!

I was too NS, too dark-skinned.

Panic time.

My gorgeous younger sister was already fixed up with an extremely cute OS whose parents didn't have a problem with his choice.

Meanwhile, our mother was making me an ice-blue satin sheath, and with my straightened and puffed up hair, black panda eyes and pale lips I would look like some third-division back-up singer for Diana Ross.

Which was the idea. We all loved Miss Ross.

But Diana couldn't help with my dilemma.

I didn't have a date.

My Mother was outraged, but not surprised.

Her own father's family are descended from Nashville OS, a family that went so far as to sometimes snub the darkerskinned members of the clan.

With Mom's beige-coloured skin and ash blonde hair she always got invited to tea at grandma's. The dark skinned ones danced to that old tune: 'If you're black, stay back'.

'Colour-struck' as we say on the South Side, a condition still rife in the black community almost everywhere and our one truly dirty little secret.

While some of us cry 'foul!' about discrimination outside of our own communities, in too many instances the dark-skinned, particularly,woman need not apply.

It's playing both sides of the street.

It didn't work back in the day and it still doesn't.

Mom dried my tears, told me that she could talk to one of her friends who had a son who played quarter back on his highschool team and was ideal (he subsequently became a go-go dancer in a gay club in New York. I loved him!), and as she continued to patiently run up the dress for me from her ubiquitous Vogue patterns, she told me about her South Side life during the War.

She went dancing as often as she could at Club DeLisa whose motto (my mother made this one up) was "everybody's the same once you walk into Club DeLisa."

She went there with our father, who used to put his best shoes in the corner and dance in his stocking feet, as nimble as a male ballet dancer.

South Side jazz musicians had a cycle of existence that kept them close to the music: your gig might end at 4 a.m; next, you would meet other musicians at The Dailey's, or the Evans Hotel Restaurant, or the little cafeteria bar at the DeLisa itself; after breakfast came the jam session at the 'Flame Lounge'; and in the early afternoon, over to a local hotel where another jam was in session; then back to your hotel room for a bit of sleep; after that another bite, drinks and by then it was night again and back to the DeLisa.

The DeLisa had a legendary house band, led for many years by Theodore Dudley 'Red' Saunders, a Chicago resident for the majority of his life.

John Phillip Sousa, the great American marching band leader who had created so much American martial music, had given a session once at Saunders highschool, and Saunders never forgot it.

After highschool, Saunders played various "walkathons' – a variation on the dance marathons held during the Depression, and best seen in the '70's movie: *They Shoot Horses, Don't They?*

Each couple walked around a track in a large sports or church hall or ballroom, day after day, taking short rest breaks, and the couple who survived won a prize bought from the entry fees of the people who watched.

Saunders kept them going.

The South Side was bristling with other clubs: 'The Annex'; 'The Claremont'; the 'Flame Lounge'; the 'Capitol Lounge'; 'The Cotton Club'.

Red started at one called 'The 29 Club' and then, until he reached the DeLisa, he worked in a club in which he had placed a bit of investment and which the black community called 'Red Saunders' Band Box', only when he left did they refer to it by its real name: 'Loop Band Box'.

Saunders worked the DeLisa with everyone: the great 'Cannonball' Adderley; the magnificent jazz baritone Joe Williams, whose voice had a chocolate quality and who left the DeLisa to work with Count Basie.

The legendary Ghanian jazz drummer Guy Warren worked with Saunders there, too. Warren was born Kpakpo Kofi Warren Gamaliel Harding Akwei and eventually became 'Kofi Ghanaba' on an album called *Africa Speaks America Answers*.

After Saunders, the house band at the DeLisa was under the direction of that future boogie-woogie piano great: Albert Ammons, but Ammons had to go because he couldn't read arrangements.

The DeLisa brothers wanted to have a floor show.

In later years, when he had returned, Saunders, would describe these shows with the 'gal'-vocalists: on the bandstand by 10, playing until 3. That would cover two shows during which the vocalist would go amongst the tables and sing, collecting tips which she would be obliged to spilt with the band.

The band had a 'runner' who followed the singers into the toilet, for fear that the women might not split the tips fairly

'Red' often got in trouble with his local musicians union simply because he needed to be practical or do things differently.

One of the unions he worked with, Local 10, was segregated and the radical musicians' union forbade other musicians to work with them.

Red had become leader of the house band at The Regal, and needed Local 10 because Josephine Baker was playing there and had demanded strings, and only the white union had string players.

The interracial camaraderie of the DeLisa came to an end with the GI Bill of 1944 which allowed returning soldiers to borrow money from banks and set up their own businesses.

The club came to an end at a breakfast dance in 1958 soon after the DeLisa brothers began to die.

The 'baby boom' was in full flow, families were young and white ex-servicemen took advantage of the prefab homes offered to them and moved to the suburbs, opening up clubs there in communities that restricted black people and sometimes Jews.

My young parents were part of this suburbanization of American culture and so they slowly accrued their own version of OS values, and set their eyes toward middle class, South Side 'Honey, I'm home' domesticity.

But they never forgot the DeLisa.

Guiding Light

Summer 2009.
Two men are arguing on cable news over the outfit that the
President chose to wear on the pitch while throwing out the last
baseball of the season.

One is arguing about the President's partisan choice of a
Chicago 'White Sox' jacket, forgetting that as a South Sider, the
Sox are his home team.

The other is complaining about his jeans: that there was a crease
down the front, that they were loose, the kind of jeans your mother
might make you wear.

The other man responds to this by calling them 'O-Mama'
jeans, not what is expected of HIM.

Not Obama.

Not cool.

Later that summer, I'm eating in a café in the shadow of the
Pompidou in Paris.

It's raining, and there's the ubiquitous low hum of Paris techno
which sounds too often like the soundtrack to some half-glimpsed
porno film/avant-garde art exhibit. The woman I'm with – impossibly Parisian, slim and picking at a boiled egg – looks up as her

husband glides in, also very chic.

He looks like the character of 'Francis' in *Round Midnight* – a film about a French guy who takes major abuse from a great black American jazz musician, played by another great jazz musician-saxophonist – Dexter Gordon. 'Francis' just wants to be with the guy, be in his aura, hang with him, because Gordon's character is the coolest guy in the world and he has deigned to allow 'Francis' to be in his presence. He has gazed upon 'Francis', crooked his finger, beckoned him. You can imagine that 'Francis' has only dreamt of this relationship from afar.

The story is lame but the music is awesome, particularly the moment when Herbie Hancock leads his band, including the great Wayne Shorter, from improvisation into making a unified sound.

Anyway, my acquaintance's husband is some big finance guy, some Master of the Universe, but all he can do is chatter like some school girl about… Barack Obama. He has a friend who's quit his job to devote himself full time to following Obama around.

As he sits down, something comes over his Blackberry from his friend – another Obamagram, another missive from the trail.

When I was growing up I knew a guy called Kirk Skolinski, his family was one of just a handful of white families who had remained in the area.

Everybody liked Kirk because he was regular and we always knew where he was coming from, and what his intentions were.

Kirk hung out with Alonzo Beasley, one of the top highschool basketball stars on the South Side.

To attain that position you had to be not only tops at the game, but cool. Very, very cool. Ice.

Believe me, everything AB did, said, or thought was cool.

He seldom smiled, but when he did it was mega-watt.

Anybody who had a problem with Kirk had to deal with AB. Kirk was brave, and devoted, too, going up against dashiki-wearing brothers in circumstances that would have been considered insane by wiser people.

Kirk had all of the records first, all of the music way ahead of any of us.

He was the first guy on the block to point out to us that *Birth Of The Cool* went way beyond being music for our parents – just as Miles Davis went way beyond being a musician for our parents.

We allowed this second-generation Pole to instruct us on the nuances of 'cool', what it meant, how to spot it, who had it.

As far as he was concerned, you could not acquire cool, and besides, the word was over-used, like 'love'. We had no exclusive right to the word just because we were who we were, just as he was not excluded from it just because he was who he was.

Kirk pointed out to us that the class conflicts between the OS and NS were bogus because Miles Davis was definitely OS and could still be for real. None of that mattered in the world of jazz, it was what you made out of yourself that counted.

Miles, he said, had arrived with his OS self to New York dressed like a man who had been brought up with servants, and as the son of a doctor, he had. Miles could go back and forth across whatever divides you wanted to create and still remain authentic, so it was best for us to put any notion that did not involve synergy out of our heads.

He talked like that to me and to Betty, and another of my girlfriends, but if we had taken that out of his basement back to our places we would have been whipped.

It was bad enough hanging out at his house, but his mother was known as a good church woman and was always there, as was his invalid grandmother.

Kirk was tiny and considered harmless, so we could be with him if we liked.

Birth of The Cool always was, and is, Kirk to me, that essence of aloofness in the music, that aloneness.

After highschool, he joined the family aluminium business in Cicero, a 'no-go' place for black people, where our dad worked, in, what I now know, had to have been trepidation in the extreme, for over four decades.

Kirk would sometimes come into town, to the Loop where I worked at a department store, under the strict supervision of a woman in a pink smock and steel-grey hair. By that time Kirk had grown a goatee and had affected a 'pimp', that South Side swagger which at its extreme can look like you have a dodgy leg when you walk. It's less extreme form is a bit like the walk Obama has at times, and which my French friend Fred calls 'immature.'

In time, Kirk's language had become even more black, a defence against Cicero I suspect, and 'motherfucker' dropped from his lips at regular intervals.

On the day that he visited me, a rather pretty lady came to the counter asking for help with some lipstick. Her face really nagged me as I helped her with various shades, and I thought that her 'goodbye' was especially warm.

After she left Kirk told me that she had been Sister Celestina, one of the nuns at our primary school, who had obviously 'leapt over the wall'.

All of the times that I had tried to imagine her without her veil and wimple flooded back into my mind, as did the times that she had taken us to see movies that the school had thought would be edifying but had turned out not to be.

Celestina would smile wryly, a very different look from the one the other nuns had, and then I could understand why.

Decades passed and I next saw Kirk at the North Sea Jazz Festival in The Hague. We had both come to see Herbie Hancock and Wayne Shorter.

I didn't speak to him. He looked as if the years had not been kind and sometimes people do not want to be reminded of the way they had been.

As I sat there watching Shorter and Herbie, Shorter walking around like a prize fighter sizing up his opponent, I looked around for Kirk.

He was down front, very quiet, while most of the rest of us were talking and moving around, thinking that the guys onstage were warming up.

But what they were doing was improvising, finding the moment to enter, and, as it suddenly dawned on me that this kind of rare beauty was happening right before our eyes, I settled down and began to understand just what jazz is.

I began to understand how Herbie painted his hometown in everything he played and composed; that Chicago thing, that feeling of power in the moment, that great sense of luxury and yearning.

When it was all over and the lights were up, Kirk was gone.

I regretted not talking to him, not telling my husband and Fred and his wife that a part of my past had been in the room.

When I was young and stupid, and thought that I had the key to jazz just because my people had brought it into being, Kirk told me about what he called the 'inner thing' and how the 'inner thing' was all. Was all anyone had.

I think what he meant, was that in standing there before us on a rainy day in Holland, Herbie and Wayne Shorter and the rest of the band were obeying an inner self – a genius that created its own attraction out into the world.

But had really nothing to do with the world.

This 'genius' – a guiding light that has its own trajectory, often manifests itself in jazz, and also is the courage of jazz musicians and people like Kirk.

Jazz has no boundaries, no constituencies.

The Estate

Obama waits with the rest of the residents of Altgeld Gardens estate. These are poor people, people who live in dire conditions. He has come to Chicago from New York to learn, to help, to find himself.

They are waiting for the director of the Chicago Housing Authority, which runs the estate.

The people have been promised this meeting after Obama, as their community organiser, went with them to the Loop to confront the official responsible for building maintenance.

They were concerned that there might be asbestos in their apartments, and they have demanded that the CHA come and reassure them.

As Obama recounts in *Dreams*, the director finally does arrive and takes the podium, but the situation sharply deteriorates.

The director leaves in a hurry, and the crowd disperses.

Obama urges them to keep trying. To keep fighting. They have turned a page. Things will change.

The young woman who had been the leader of the protestors listens respectfully and then tells Obama that her sole goal now is to save money.

So that she can move away.

The Chicago housing estates, known as 'the projects' – where, for the most part, failed social experiments that failed were, in some instances, attempts to find decent housing for the poor. But because of the housing situation in Chicago and the way that the neighbourhoods had been populated, the housing ended up racially segregated. They became 'no go' areas. They became ghettos.

The main public housing estate on the South Side when we moved to Ruby Avenue was called the 'Robert Taylor Homes.'

I never knew who Robert Taylor was when I lived on Ruby Avenue, but I've since discovered that he was a black activist who worked for the Chicago Housing Authority in 1950 and resigned because the CHA would not work for racially diverse housing.

Robert Taylor was made up of 28 high-rise buildings, 16 stories each.

There were 4,321 apartments arranged in U-shaped clusters of three, stretching for two miles (three kilometers) in total.

The estate was completed in Bronzeville in 1962 with good intentions. But it is not possible to squeeze that many human beings together and expect the best results. Life there could, at times, be on the scale of what used to be called 'the Third World.'

Inspite of the conditions, great, decent people found a way to live in respect and peace and pride.

The present governor of Massachusetts, Deval Patrick, came from Robert Taylor.

Robert Taylor is gone now, low rise developments replace it.

One of my brothers lives in its environs in a lovely apartment that would not have been imaginable when we were growing up.

It is close to the Loop and so, as these things go, urban-dwellers are moving in: the professionals, and the artists, and those who want to live somewhere a little bit different.

You have to wonder where all of the people of Robert Taylor have gone.

We never lived in a housing project, but our mother's childhood friend did.

They were and still are very close.

We called her 'auntie' and her children were our 'cousins'.

They lived in another project, Henry Horner, located on the Near West Side underneath the elevated train track on Lake Street.

That elevated train became like a coda in my life.

I would sit beneath the big blue-eyed painting of Jesus, that Aunt Cary adored and whose eyes followed you everywhere, and listen for that elevated train. Going somewhere. Going somewhere.

Sixteen stories below my cousins' apartment was the play-ground.

At first you would think that you need the eyes of an eagle to spot your child down that far, but you always knew who was yours.

You could develop your lungs to a high degree shouting at the children down below. Summoning away yours from the steel slide or the broken swings.

I knocked a tiny hole in the back of my head falling off the jungle gym on that concrete playground.

I suppose that hole explains a lot.

We were South Siders by then and the trek west was difficult but our mother insisted that we make it.

'Aunt' Cary's husband, 'Uncle' Bill, was a kind of community organiser.

He was always trying to get the boys into the local organization, The Better Boys Foundation, and away from the gangs.

He didn't always succeed, but he was greatly respected. Everyone did their best.

When JFK was assassinated we kids became obsessed by the funeral drum, that solemn, grieving pattern that we beat on the windows as the adults cried.

We cried, too, because we thought that we might suffer in some way, and the little ones thought that we were all going back into slavery.

At Henry Horner, there were the usual horrible housing estate events; rapes, muggings, murders.

Once a friend of Aunt Cary's lost her only son in the lift, the one that never worked properly and suddenly one night, had lurched into life, sending everyone in it crashing to the bottom.

The police came, the ambulances. But there was no investigation. Nothing happened.

We all knew it would be that way.

People cried but none of us spoke about it.

The walls of the apartment were made of concrete and were hard and cold and sometimes they 'wept', streams of water pouring down them.

There must have been asbestos in the place, too, the kind of situation that Obama fought in Altgeld Gardens, but if someone came to help Henry Horner, I didn't know about it.

There was a basement at the bottom of the building, a part of the place that no one ventured into.

Rumours abounded of mutant rats living there, rats as big as dogs, and feral cats, prehistoric and wild.

Now that the estate is gone, maybe it was discovered that these were simply urban myths.

And maybe not.

Uncle Bill especially was a massive fan of the comedian Dick Gregory.

Gregory was and still is a huge talent, who influenced Lenny Bruce all the way down to Chris Rock with a detour to Richard Pryor. He changed the way that white people saw black people.

Gregory never laughed or grinned.

He came out in slender suits, like a Wall Street Mad Man.

He had started out as a promising track star at a university in downstate Illinois, but quickly understood that they were not interested in educating him. They just wanted him to run.

He had been a comedian in the Army and after realizing that he was wasting his time at university, he moved upstate to Chicago to try his luck there on the comedy circuit.

Consider this: before Dick Gregory there had been largely the minstrel tradition or variations on that theme. I had grown up watching a television show called *Amos And Andy* – two 'negroes' invented for radio and played by two white men. But it wasn't on to black-up on television by the '50's, so black people played the parts. By the time I got stuck into the box as a little kid in the late '50's, *Amos And Andy* was a major hit. The story was set in Harlem and featured a country bumpkin named Amos, a wise taxi driver called Andy; and the Kingfish, a wily lawyer out to steal from anyone he could. Complementing this trio were a battleaxe mother-in-law known as Mamma, and

Sapphire, a name that entered the lexicon of black speech in times gone by and stood for the negative, bitchy, angry, hollering black woman.

To be referred to as a 'Sapphire' was highly insulting and could be the source of serious bodily harm.

The humour of *Amos And Andy* was broad, lots of shucking and jiving, eye-popping and gurning.

As a kid I thought it was brilliant.

For me, it was like watching a bunch of adults act like little children.

But for the adults it was ghastly and with what was going on in the South, *Amos And Andy* had to go.

Then, out of the blue – as if the age itself had called him – came Dick Gregory.

Gregory was a Chicago postal worker by day and played Roberts Show Lounge on the South Side by night.

One evening Hugh Hefner walked in and heard the following:

"Good evening ladies and gentlemen.

"I understand there are a good many Southerners in the room tonight. I know the South very well. I spent twenty years there one night.

"Last time I was down South I walked into this restaurant and this white waitress came up to me and said, 'We don't serve coloured people here.' I said, 'That's all right. I don't eat coloured people. Bring me a whole fried chicken.'

"Then these three white boys came up to me and said, 'Boy, we're givin' you fair warnin'. Anything you do to that chicken, we're gonna do to you'.

"So I put down my knife and fork, I picked up that chicken and I kissed it.

"Then I said, 'Line up, boys!'"

Gregory was not only a revelation, he was a revolution.

This would go down well in Hef's cool scene on the North Side at the Playboy Club, and Dick Gregory was booked to replace Professor Irwin Corey, an absent-minded professor routine.

From there he became THE star of observational comedy and went on to publish his autobiography *Nigger*.

He told black people if they heard the 'n' word directed at them that it was advertising for his book and to make sure that whoever said it bought a copy.

He went on to name one of his ten children 'Miss' so that, he pointed out, no one would ever call her by her first name, that act of disrespect which could still be suffered by black women no matter what age they were.

Not his child.

In whatever circumstances she might find herself, she would always be 'Miss Gregory.'

In 1968, he ran for President and made more sense than anyone else who ran.

He's still around, and if it wasn't for Gregory, a lot of folks in Henry Horner and other housing estates in Chicago, including the Gardens, would have had life that much tougher.

And at the same time that Dick Gregory was doing the business at Roberts Show Lounge, Oscar Brown Jr. entered the scene.

Oscar was a South Sider, through and through. He looked like a South Sider: turned out in dapper dress, a bit louche, a touch of Africa, but above all clothed in all of the wisdom of the South that came from his ancestors.

I suppose if you wanted to label him, you could have called him OS: his dad, Oscar Brown Sr. was a successful real estate dealer and attorney.

Oscar attended Englewood, one of my highschool's mortal rivals, and several universities without obtaining a degree.

He served a while in the U.S. Army which was officially segregated until 1948, when by Truman's Presidential degree, it was un-segregated.

While in the Army, he expressed certain views about the condition of black people that did not go down very well, and he was accused of being a Communist, a great way to get yourself inside a jail cell.

He was all set up to become a lawyer like his dad, but that great gospel diva, Mahalia Jackson recorded one of his songs and he was on his way.

He became so well-known, was such a virtuoso, that by 1960, when he released his first album, Nina Simone and Lorraine Hansberry, amongst others, wrote the liner notes.

Miss Simone went on to record his *Work Song* and made it into a classic.

Work Song is very Oscar, very South Side: that combination of remembrance of the cotton field, and the rail road track, and the lash and the lynching rope; mixed with a citified-insouciance, a jauntiness lurking just underneath, tucked away inside the beat.

His song: *But I Was Cool* is a magnificent send-up of the uber-cool black guy, keeping his cool, black man thing together to the point of absurdity, sung in a minimalist jazz style.

Signifyin' Monkey takes the mythical monkey in African mythology who harasses you with home truths and puts a jaunty, walking jazz sound to it.

And there were his musicals, particularly *Kicks & Co* about a slick, urban South Side devil.

He was the South Side's own Serge Gainsborough in the pro-liferation of his song-writing (he wrote over a 1,000) and he was like the great Sammy Davis Jr. too, in that he was a song and dance man, and knew what that was all about.

Oscar stayed with the people as much as he could, and once, outside Henry Horner, there was a palpable buzz in the concrete courtyard. The buzz this time was for a GOOD reason, not a bad one.

Oscar was down there with his beautiful daughter 'Africa', come to see a local show.

I did not see this happen myself because I had moved to New York by that time, but I heard that Oscar signed autographs, posed for photos, whatever the people wanted.

I once met up with him when I was trying to get him pro-duced in New York by Joe Papp, who I worked for. We sat in a restaurant in South Shore.

It was the early '80's and Oscar was tired, but his eyes danced and he was writing more songs.

The lake was behind him and somehow that image of him seemed to capture something about transcendence for me, something about the way forward.

He always looked ahead, was always optimistic, was always ready and willing to do it again.

He was simply a genius, a South Side genius, and like Dick Gregory, he brought something called sharpness and ease to the scene.

He made the people feel 'Yes We Can'.

Sitting By The Door

It is a few days before the election and the Democratic candidate has decided to walk with his daughter, Sasha, to his neighbour's house for the annual 'trick or treat' party.

He's done this before and he will do it this time, hand in hand with his little 'corpse bride'.

The press, the paparazzi, are in hot pursuit, clogging the tight sidewalk.

The most famous person on earth begs them to leave him and his little daughter in peace.

Soon, trick or treaters by their hundreds are converging on his neighbour's house, a man none too happy that his friend has decided to walk down the street, alerting the world to his home.

Finally inside, Obama asks one question: whether he will ever be able to do this again.

The day before he moves to Washington to take the Oath of Office as 44th President of the United States he sits alone in his empty house.

Michelle, her mother – Mrs. Robinson, and the girls have all moved to Washington ahead of him.

A neighbour has dropped off an album of photos.

He opens the album. Looks at the photos.

And cries.

He is about to become the spook who sits INSIDE.

A few months later, at the opening of the New Acropolis Museum in Athens. On a tour of the Museum, I notice a gorgon, a monster with negroid features.

In ancient Greece, the gorgon's purpose was to be: '... grim of aspect, glaring terribly, causing Terror and Rout'.

Terror and rout.

The forces that change sometimes unleash.

Sometimes must unleash.

Was that what was happening deep down in the American psyche in this summer of 2009?

As a student, with the little money I would have left over after paying my university fees, I would sometimes go to what was called 'Greek Town'.

The food was inexpensive and good, and when we could afford it, my friends and I would move up and down the street, one restaurant for starters, one for the main course, one for dessert, one for coffee and a drink.

From the Greek restaurant, I could take food home and it could last a few days, and keep me going for awhile. It was a recession then, too, but we were much too young to know what that meant. Besides, I had never had any money and therefore couldn't miss it now.

Before one of our excursions, one of my South Side friends called me, knowing that I did this Greek Town thing once in awhile, and asked if she could come and bring along her uncle.

Old Uncle Phil. I knew who she meant.

He was in and out of the veteran's hospital with an old war wound from Korea. And other stuff.

He had lived on the West Side, in and out of various people's homes.

But when his mother – my friend's grandmother died – he suddenly changed, and moved out south to the family home.

Uncle Phil began to paint and weed and clean, and greeted everyone he saw with a glorious smile. But the man had ghosts. The Korean War had done that to Uncle Phil.

Sometimes he could be seen walking briskly up and down the street, as if he was in a hurry, but no one knew to where.

Saturday nights, religiously from 9 to 1, he played at top volume the most furious bebop. He would turn it down if anyone complained, wait a half an hour, then turn it up again.

Uncle Phil was from a strange military generation – the one right after World War Two, my Dad's time, and long before Vietnam, my time.

These three wars were different worlds for the soldier of African descent.

Vietnam was just beginning the night of that dinner, which went down in legend as the 'Uncle Phil Moment'.

Gradually, we came to understand who he was and where he had been.

On July 26, 1948, a month after the 'Windrush' had docked at Tilbury, changing Britain forever, President Truman signed Executive Order 9981.

This Order de-segregated the military and ordered equality of opportunity and treatment within it.

This desegregation took years to bring about. Uncle Phil, and other black GIs still fought in all-black units in Korea.

In 1950, a black corporal, Leon Gilbert was court-martialled and sentenced to death for refusing the command of a white officer to take his men into certain death.

The case led to world-wide protest and as a result his sentence was commuted to twenty years, then seventeen, then five, and then he was released.

The Executive Order extended to the community of the military: schools, neighbourhoods, hospitals.

It also imposed an 'off-limits' obligation on the commanding officer, i.e. there could be no racial segregation on the base or around it, even off-duty.

Because of these stipulations, it took up until 1970 – a few years before the Uncle Phil meal – before the Order could be fully realized after it was implemented.

Uncle Phil, like one of my own uncles, was a hipster, a jive cat.

Everybody was 'man', said in that elongated way and followed by a sly laugh, as if he were about to go into a furious scat solo.

That evening, he drank too much retsina and gave us a lecture.

As far as he was concerned, the most important couple of minutes in 20th Century music can be heard on Charlie Parkers's album: *Cool Bird*.

With Charlie himself on alto sax; the young Miles Davis on trumpet; Duke Jordan on piano; Tommy Potter on double bass; and Max Roach on drums, this album sliced 'swing' – the dominant music of the time – up and threw it away.

We youngsters were bringing swing back in the form of the Pointer Sisters and Bette Midler, but a lot of that was camp and missed Uncle Phil's point.

The dictionary says that the word 'bebop' can be considered to have come from scat starting with the great Charlie Christian mumbling the word as he played; from Dizzie Gillespie, according to him the audience would yell 'bebop' when they wanted him to play something but they had forgotten the name; from Latin American bandleaders as a form of 'Ariba! Arriba!' (*'Vaya arriba!'* – 'get on with it!'); from mid-'40's r'n'b; from Gene Vincent's song *Be-Bop-A Lua*; and of course, *bop, bop, a re-bop*, which you can hear in most '40's films with any jazz in them, like the jazz club flash-sequence in 1946's multi-Oscar winner about returning soldiers: *The Best Years Of Our Lives*.

Dizzy and Bird had come out of Chicago after playing with masters like Earl Hines and Jack Teagarden.

They started exploring harmony, syncopation, chords, and pushed what they found to another level and away from the comfortable 'easy listening' niche that jazz had become.

Swing usually used big orchestras, bebop was small.

Bebop took a theme ('a head') – usually a standard, i.e. a well-known pop or jazz tune – given to the audience at the beginning and the end, and the improvisation ('riffs') were in between.

It was super fast, intricate, asymmetrical and used the rhythm section way beyond being merely the watch mechanism of the band.

Harmonies were complex, dissonant, free.

Bebop was – and is – beautiful.

On *Cool Bird* Parker lays bebop on top of the Gershwin classic *Embraceable You*, taking it into another dimension of reality.

You have to listen to it for awhile and then gradually you can hear the theme tune being built underneath what Bird and Miles and Max Roach are laying down, sounding as if they have just made up *Embraceable You* right then and there.

Even today, if you give it time, it can still sound fresh, still sound amazing.

Cool Bird broke new ground because, finally, a new generation of jazz had emerged and found its voice. And that voice was the voice of the black soldier, yearning – demanding – to be free.

He was taking his freedom.

To Uncle Phil, Sarah Vaughn was the chocolate goddess with that contralto that made bebop into a woman.

He wanted Shirley Scott, the organist and queen of hardbop, to play at his funeral.

To him bebop – and hardbop – were all that mattered.

He was obsessed with liberating Wes Montgomery from the 'cool and mellow' label that he had begun to acquire.

To him, the late great Wes Montgomery was hardbop, and like all hardbop musicians, he had brought jazz back to church and back to the field, back to foot-stomping and inner call and response with his thumb on those strings and the insistence of the beat.

Wes had brought it back from the cerebral regions into which some bebop players had taken the music by the late '50's.

Thanks to France and Japan and Britain, he would say

By the time the music lecture had ended, Uncle Phil's face had softened and become puffy from drink, and his eyes had become watery and lost.

Invisible Man, he concluded, could be considered the ultimate bebop, black existentialist novel. But the author Ralph Ellison would not have thanked Uncle Phil for saying this.

The novel is about a black man who sees himself as invisible. He lives in a whites-only 19th Century building in New York, in the forgotten basement part, lit by 1,369 lights. The story is told in flashback, ending with the man back where he started, but with the knowledge that stories must be told and reclaimed, light must be stolen from the top.

Ellison himself detested the new music for its disavowal of Louis Armstrong and its growing pretension and movement toward the European avant-garde.

Garlanded with awards and feted until the end, Ellison was NS,dug into his roots, and bebop, to him, had forgotten where it came from.

Ellison was a master, Uncle Phil said, but we had one right here too, alive, and writing in bebop's dark, satirical vein – like a Mingus with a pen, Charlie Parker on a typewriter – Sam Greenlee. Greenlee had written a novel called *The Spook Who Sat By The Door* which had not been able to get a publisher in the States, but had been published in Britain by a young black British writer/publisher called Margaret Busby, and her partner, to great acclaim and sales.

Busby, he said, had brought a Chicago reality to the world, plus he had seen her picture and he was anxious to meet her.

The title 'spook' refers to a spy, but is also a derogatory term, in the States, for a black person, so it has a double meaning. The 'sat by the door' part refers to an affirmative action technique of putting black people in reception or as greeters, but not inside of the organization itself, not near the decision-making apparatus.

Greenlee may have been in intelligence himself, but what he captures is that time in Chicago – the late '60's – a time of uprisings, of re-definition, of flux.

It was a world in which the paradigm of power did not include anyone like himself, or Uncle Phil, or any of us sitting around that table in the Greek Restaurant, drinking wine with an old man.

Later, Uncle Phil caught a Greyhound bus south and into oblivion.

I later learned that he himself had been one of those 'spooks', an accountant who had been hired by a big downtown firm after he had passed his exams.

They had wanted a vet, and a black person to be on their books and in their annual report. But they had given him nothing substantive to do. Instead he had honed his knowledge and love for bebop and jazz on the side streets of the Loop where he would walk into record shops and browse and listen to the old timers talk.

The music had finally done its work and set him free.

It had made him no longer content to sit by the door.

All The Things You Could Be By Now if Sigmund Freud's Wife Was Your Mother

The White House, mid June, 2009.

The Associated Press reports that 150 talented young jazz musicians are in the house to 'celebrate an original American art form'.

First Lady Michelle Obama tells the gathering that her grandfather had put speakers into every room of his house and would play jazz all day long.

AP quotes her as saying "At Christmas, birthdays, Easter. It didn't matter. There was jazz playing in our household."

And AP also states that the President is the nation's Number One jazz fan.

The event takes place during the Duke Ellington Jazz Festival, Washington DC's biggest music event.

The Marsalis family: father Ellis, sons Jason, Delfeayo, Branford and Wynton are there, too, dispensing tips, teaching the music, extending the tradition.

'There's probably no better example of democracy than a jazz ensemble: individual freedom, but with responsibility to the group.'

The event ends with Wynton Marsalis playing, with other musicians, a version of Dizzy Gillespie's classic: *A Night In Tunisia*.

One young musician expresses shock and awe at being in the White House.

She says this: that she never expected anyone like her to be there at all.

'*Wurf*'.

Heidegger places the human condition into this German word that translates as 'thrownness'– the state of dice after they are thrown.

Heidegger believes that there is, in the end, nothing that exists to tell you what life is about.

It is all '*wurf*.'

That same summer of 2009.

I am reading in *The Guardian* a story about all of the gun crime on the South Side, the number of children being killed.

It is written in astonishment and sorrow.

But what does this writer expect?

Does he they think that this is new?

Why does this story even exist?

Because these catastrophes are taking place in Obama's neighbourhood?

What does anyone think can happen when people are walled in, when that walled-in-ness settles into the DNA? When men are coming of age in a masculine-dominated society in which they cannot be men, here there is no reflection of them in the media for the most part, except a negative one?

Is it because these things are now happening with children, with ten year olds, that age of genius and separation?

How can you become visible in a society and a culture where you are invisible, except through streaks of lightning?

All of us on the black South Side have sat in, or known someone who has sat in, a pew near the casket of a child killed in the streets.

You live with death like you live with life. There's no word to explain what that condition is. Only music.

The article states that there are those in the community and outside who complain that the President must say something, make a gesture, indicate that he will do something about all of this.

But may I respectfully submit to these people that perhaps the man has decided to do something.... to go to the top ...because the bottom is so crowded, so stifling.

Just be up there, be seen, and in being seen effect a solution, a change.

A new music.

This is what I think anyway, for what it's worth.

A new music. That's what the word 'straight-ahead' means in jazz.

Abbey Lincoln was born in Chicago, and there are few jazz women who have been more relentlessly straight ahead than this maestra.

She is in the tradition, makes tradition, and breaks it, too, all at once.

You can hear bits of Billie Holiday in her voice, Billie if she had lived a longer, more beautiful life.

Abbie Lincoln sometimes wears a kind of top hat, or maybe it's a conjurer's hat, and always combines the political with art, which, I suspect for Ms. Lincoln are the same thing.

She is a vocalist, like Billie Holiday and Sinatra in that she is talking to you, straight from the heart, and the words come out musically, that's all.

As young teens, we cried our eyes out during the film of *Nothing But A Man* in which she played a woman trying to help her husband make sense of his life, and we smiled when she did a romantic lead with Sidney Poitier in *For Love Of Ivy*.

She was beautiful and straightforward as an actor, but as a musician she can take you through the sinews of pain and truth. When she was married to Max Roach, they were, for me: 'AbbeyLincolnMaxRoach' – one person – and that is, at some level, the pantheon in which she remains.

Through her and others, Edlita and I were discovering our own beauty apart from what was being shown to us on television.

Which was – as it remains today – not very much.

Mixed in, in my inner world, with Ms. Lincoln and all of the truth that she embodies, was the gilded world of the Playboy Mansion.

A family on Ruby Avenue had a daughter working at the Playboy Club. We thought that this was fabulous. All of us girls knew all about it.

That original Playboy Mansion was 70 rooms of play, on North State Parkway on the Gold Coast.

Built in 1899, Hef had bought it in 1959. By the time we were dreaming of it, about 5 years later, it was at the height of its glory and the height of cool.

Girls not much older than us tottered around on vertiginous heels, wearing bunny ears and living on the exotic North Side, another world.

Good Catholic girls or not, we wanted to be there, in the glamour.

And being a great lover of Latin, I was pleased to learn a few years later that Hef had inscribed on the mansion's door: *Si Non*

Oscillas, Noli Tintinnare ('If you don't swing, don't ring').

Not far away from the Mansion was the elegant epicentre of Chicago jazz: Rush Street.

There are bridges across the Chicago River that remind me of being in Venice.

We could only see Rush Street from our family cars on Sundays, the façade of the clubs, the darkened lights of the street that shone bright at night.

But the Mansion and Rush Street were the capitals of smooth jazz.

We grew through our adolescence with smooth jazz.

The down tempo.

Melody-lead, easily recognisable.

On some level, for us, Wes Montgomery and Ahmad Jamal, the music of our parents to a certain extent, was 'smooth'.

This was a mark of our ignorance, but this is what I mean:

Wes Montgomery was born in Indianapolis, Indiana, right across the line from the South Side of Chicago.

It was where he died, too, in the city where the great stock car race is held, the 'Indianapolis 500', the working class Formula One.

He learned everything that he could from the great Charlie Christian and he learned by ear. He played with his thumb instead of a pick, and his thumb was special. George Benson says that he was double-jointed, he could bend it all the way back, plus it had a strategically placed corn which could give him a unique sound, since the corn was his very own, made in its own way.

Master of masters, learners try to copy him. He played with Miles and with Wynton Kelly and there are those who say that when he moved away from the innovation, things declined into populism.

I think that my father must have played Ahmad Jamal's *Live At the Pershing* every Sunday afternoon, after lunch. I know it by heart.

He was leader of the house trio at the Pershing Room down town, a fantastic coup, and although the pressure of his fingers on the keyboard makes him technically hardbop, (as it does Montgomery, by the way), his sensibility is 'smooth', at least at The Pershing Room, that title of the album of his that I carry in my mind and heart to this day.

Edlita fled the South Side after highschool.

Her big brother had been killed by a gang, but at the funeral the family had discovered that his death was more like an assassination, a hit, because the gang had showed up to pay homage, taking over the proceedings, leaving everyone helpless and in shock.

She attended university and took up Black Lit as a way to understand what had happened to her brother.

Being Edlita, she did not do the conventional thing, but took up a kind of Zen approach, the 'Not This'.

Or, in other words, she used a kind of '*reductio ab absurdam*' technique, a method of logic where you work through what a problem 'is not' until you are left with something you cannot work through – and that logically must be the answer you are looking for.

The is.

She started with *The Man*, a potboiler about the consequences of having the first black President of the United States.

The irony of the title is that, in black parlance, 'the man' is the white man, the guy in charge.

Through a series of highly improbable incidents, the black President pro tempore of the Senate becomes President of the

United States after the President and the Speaker of the House (number three in line for the Presidency) are both killed, and the Vice-President refuses the job.

This black man, Douglas Dilman, becomes Job, of course suffering all things for all men up to and including the fact that he has a daughter passing for white – the ultimate offence.

By the way, a Constitutional Amendment was passed shortly after the novel was published, and before the film version came out, nailing down the succession to the Presidency because that had not been formally determined before.

I suppose that no one wanted 'The Man' to happen for real!

Norman Mailer's incendiary late '50's essay *The White Negro: Superficial Reflections on the Hipster* was next on her list, an essay which took apart those whites who dressed like black people, thought themselves to be black people, and could, therefore, live like black people did, and feel what black people felt. They thought.

Through Mailer's eyes, she tried to see what he saw, and extricate pieces of herself and of her dead brother from the observation of The Other.

Soon she went the other away and read Amiri Baraka's novel *The System Of Dante's Hell* in which Baraka rebuilds the 'Inferno' in black Newark, New Jersey, on the edge of the explosion in the racial cauldron that was the '60's.

This novel lead her to the music of Rahssan Roland Kirk because she liked to hear the sound of his breathing and the hums that he made when he performed with Charles Mingus. Plus he made jokes about the black condition onstage with the freedom of a Mingus.

She rang me from O'Hare one rainy day when I lived in the

back of a furniture shop because I had no money for a flat and couldn't afford to live on campus.

She was on her way out of the country, she said.

She just needed some air.

That breath of air has lasted for almost three decades.

Years later I received a scribbled note and a photo of Edlita with a funny – looking little Frenchman, whom I was convinced she had wed in a '*marriage blanc*' until Noire was born nine months to the day after their wedding. Edlita became deeply involved with raising her daughter and insuring she – in Edlita's words – stayed 'coloured', by taking her to have fried chicken at Leroy Haynes' restaurant on a regular basis, and attending the writers' talks at Shakespeare and Co. whenever a black American was in town.

In time she woke up and divorced the French husband, but got joint ownership of his family apartment on the isle St. Louis, in sight of Notre Dame and the sound of its bells.

She earned extra money for Noire's school fees by advertising the flat in American lit journals for those who thought that Paris and American equalled Scott Fitzgerald and not Edlita's cold-as-a-tomb in winter and hot-as-a-sauna in summer apartment.

Because of Noire, Paris had become better.

She had fallen in love with a much younger man, a Surinamese guy based in Amsterdam but who came often to Paris to work.

She knew that Leo was mainly interested in the possibility of a Green Card and, in the fullness of time, an American passport, because he planned to commute between New York and Chicago and become as rich and as famous as he could.

Leo read Stanley Crouch, who had enough poetic grace and devil-take-the-highroad to interchange 'Negro', 'negro', and 'black' without fear because he knew that a name is not what it describes.

Edlita moved Leo into the apartment near Notre Dame.

There he could imagine himself a Baudelaire in dreads.

He re-paid her generosity with violence and turmoil through 'straight ahead', which he considered Chicago to be the capital of, no matter what anyone else said.

'Straight-ahead.'

Ornette Coleman, Charles Mingus, Sun Ra – to name a few – made music which the ordinary jazz fan would, at times, consider un-listenable.

For Leo these fans were always listening for the known and for reassurance, not willing to push the boundaries of the music, of their own lives, and those people he wished to have nothing to do with.

His gods were the Association For The Advancement Of Creative Musicians.

The AACM, straight out of Chicago, who had burst the town open so wide that they had had to move to New York where there was an ocean and the possibility of more space for the music to be contained in.

Instead of Wes Montgomery's dulcet and complex tones, Leo preferred 'shred' guitar.

'Shred', as far as he was concerned, was the thing to take it all forward.

He loved listening to MAB – Michael Angelo Batio – whom he intended to join up with as soon as he reached Chicago.

Not having been blessed with MAB's ambidexterity – his ability to play two guitars at once – nor his speed and general genius on the instrument, Leo intended to sit at his feet and absorb what he felt was the essence of Chicago caught in the strings of an artist.

Edlita tried her best to move into what – to her ears – sounded like rock guitar 'dive-bombing' and Ted Nugent type antics, she was so obsessed with Leo that she tried her best to learn.

She had never experienced the Chicago that MAB described in his work or that Leo was building in his mind.

From there he ushered her into Eddie Van Halen, and just as she was becoming thoroughly confused, he brought in Yuseff Lateef.

Dr. Lateef is a composer, a music educator and a virtuoso on many instruments, many of them Eastern, like the Japanese traditional string instrument, the koto. He dislikes the term 'jazz' itself. Being a devout Muslim and man of the spirit, his theory of 'autophys-iopsychic music' – music which emanates from the entire being – is too big a subject to contain within a small word like 'jazz'.

This tortured Leo from time to time, and when it did, he would open the small metal suitcase, which would cause him trouble at border crossings, but which he never allowed to leave his sight while travelling. It contained his small collection of original albums under the Impulse! label, ie. the works of Yuseff Lateef; Freddie Hubbard; Pharaoh Saunders; Archie Shepp; Sun Ra; McCoy Tyner, Alice Coltrane, and her husband, John.

He told Edlita that he played Coltrane's *A Love Supreme* every-day as a form of prayer and Charles Mingus, who had also been on Impulse!, as his guide to life.

Edlita listened and tried to learn because she was in love, but nothing could prepare her for Mingus.

How could he tell her that there was nothing to prepare her.

Mingus was hard to explain without listening to the music and even then, old things had to be discarded and new things taken on with great speed.

Mingus had taken on the governor of Arkansas, Orville Faubus, who had tried to keep a group of black highschool students from attending the school of their choice in the '50's.

While the world watched in outrage, as the howling mobs surrounded the demure students day after day, and Faubus sat at his desk day after day, in the governor's mansion, a huge American flag draped behind him, extolling the right of his state of Arkansas to do what it damn well pleased, Mingus was creating a piece of music called *Fables Of Faubus*.

His bass is actually laughing at the man, mocking him.

Jaunty and light, but menacing, too, the tune has come down through time without many people knowing its daring origin.

Goodbye Pork Pie Hat, a tribute to the jaunty hat placed at a rakish angle that many black men wore in the '50's and signified a freedom they did not have, is mournful and nostalgic.

The thing that Leo loved about Mingus, above all, and which he tried to emulate was the fact that Mingus did not care.

Mingus did not live anyone else's life but his own, which he had dedicated himself to with a great religiosity.

He listened to no one but himself and would not allow the old templates, the why-things-had-always-been-and-would-always-be to define him.

Nothing depended on whether others understood him, but everything on whether he was getting right what he heard and felt because life was short and everyone was going to catch the same train.

He worked with great speed because he understood the inertia of human beings.

Leo particularly liked *All The Things You Could Be By Now if*

Sigmund Freud's Wife Was Your Mother because of its exploding, frantic horns, Mingus' riffing – his running up and down his bass, bleating like Miles could, the music like a traffic jam, and the bass player as leader.

Mingus. A man of many 'races' blended in his face and in his mind, a man who broke free and stayed free, who called his autobiography *Beneath The Underdog* and who had his ashes scattered in The Ganges.

Through Mingus, Leo had become obsessed with Obama after seeing his photo in a newspaper and feeling that there was something of Mingus in him.

Mingus in particular and 'straight-ahead' in general had taught him that if someone was born at the right time in history, in the right place, and in the right circumstances, then what looked to be a 'miracle' on the outside could occur.

The world had been ready for *Fables Of Faubus* because, underneath the horror of watching the chief law officer of a state defy the law, there was something laughable and absurd about the man trying to hold back the ocean of history.

Obama had been born to be where he was right now, and he had made his progress like a man walking on stones leading across the water to the other side.

All it took was intelligence, drive, courage – both physical and moral – and a burning self-belief.

Noire rings me in London to catch up and to talk about a new hip hop group that she has discovered in the suburbs of Paris who combine rap with scat and a bepop attitude.

I love the portal of hip hop – the gateways and doors that it opens, the bridges that it builds, the feelings and thoughts that it can translate.

But Noire is her mother's child, a South Sider in her bones and a child of jazz.

In the end, everything is music and you either know that and live accordingly or you don't know that and live accordingly.

Noire mentions in passing that she thinks that the 44th President of the United States is a kind of metaphor for music itself, and jazz in particular.

She asks me to give this some thought

I say that I will.

Ancient To The Future

In the summer of '09, a headline on an American website reads: 'Calling All Crazies. Obama needs you.'

It asks the question: what good is facing the enemy when all they want to do is pose with you?

One woman cannot even ask a question because: 'the President winked at me.'

And there is a postcard floating around that reads: 'Socialized medicine scares me a lot less than the people scared of socialized medicine' complete with a cartoon of a caveman.

Brussels, later in the summer of '09.
I am standing outside of a shop in the centre.

The windows are full of flat screen televisions showing the President at a town hall meeting.

Could it be?

The old demon race, – this time in the guise of fear of the President's health plan, is rearing its ugly head? So soon...

Yes, I know that many, probably even most of the people, screaming at the town hall meetings are sincere and anxious.

But why are they mainly all white?

Is it because people 'of colour' have no health insurance

to protect?

Is this just a coincidence, nothing to be alarmed about?

But I am.

Where are the Hispanics, Native Americans, where are they in these groups?

The old fear is coming back.

Somebody, wheel some of them in front of the camera so that I don't start thinking what I don't want to think.

Please.

I never accepted the 'post racial' stuff.

I live outside the matrix, I could see what it looked like over there, even in the midst of the hoopla, the joy.

Am I being unpatriotic even thinking like this?

What country do I owe allegiance to?

To the one that I was born in, grew up in, still consider myself to be a part of, still love and miss deeply in my rackety way?

Or the one which I've given allegiance to, my native land would say to a 'foreign prince, a nation and a people which has allowed me to grow, find love and acceptance and respect and joy? A nation whose memorial service and the tolling of Big Ben on Remembrance Sunday still makes me cry, because, although America lost many in World War One, it did not lose its innocence.

Or is my nation 'another country' as James Baldwin named it. A nation that I am building myself, inside and outside?

A friend from the South Side, who moved to Dallas from New Orleans after Hurricane Katrina, is standing outside the shop beside me.

Duke has been supporting the President since 2002 and he is not happy now.

Neither am I.

I stand there listening to Barack's speech.

I think that the President looks a bit greyer.

He's been sitting too much, he's a tiny bit heavier at the bottom.

Maybe this is inevitable, this is the real world.

He doesn't belong to me, he isn't the 'black' President.

He has to be there for everybody.

But I can't help it.

I think about his spokespeople, his advisors, his Cabinet.

I know that they're good people, effective people, smart people.

But I just wish that he had more South Siders with him, like the women from Altgeld Gardens who rode downtown with him and stood up to the bureaucrats.

I want to see the brothers from 'Smitty's' step up to the microphone in the Rose Garden and tell people what the President thinks.

This is ridiculous of me, wrong.

I mustn't and cannot assume that these things matter to him because they matter to me, that maybe my existence and that of my friends has been a pathology in the end, no matter how many theories I wrap around it.

What difference does any of it make if you're not living your own life, and isn't it some kind of 'point of view?'

I think, like some kind of big sister, that he should stop talking, be invisible, burn that midnight oil in the Oval Office.

Like Miles would have said of Louis Armstrong: 'Don't smile so much.'

We haven't said anything, but Duke concurs.

He suddenly says that in Dallas he's learned an old cowboy expression:

'Never miss an opportunity to shut up.'

Brussels is under construction and we are walking around rubble.

I tell Duke over coffee in Grande Place what another South Sider who lives here tells me: that Belgium is broken, divided, the centre of power does not reside in its capital. Where is Europe going, she wonders.

Duke is here, first of all to see his Air Force daughter attached to NATO, and secondly to attend the North Sea Jazz Festival.

His daughter is so proud to have the President's picture all over the place, so proud that she can say that the Commander-in-chief knows her life, how she grew up.

Who she is. What she wants to do.

Duke wants to get back to Rotterdam and find Ahmed Aboualeb, the mayor, shake his hand.

Born 3 weeks after the President, Aboualeb is called the 'Obama Of The Netherlands' and Duke is fascinated by this dual citizen of The Netherlands and Morocco, and a practicing Muslim.

Duke likes what he is and what he represents.

To him, Rotterdam is a good 'coloured' town: West Indian, Turkish, Moroccan and the indigenous Dutch. A good model for Europe.

He pops one of his heart pills and shakes his head as Obama walks across the White House lawn.

Duke still can't believe it.

The tears still come.

I think of the ride on the tour bus that I had taken earlier in the summer, in June.

I had not seen before how baroque the centre of Brussels is. On that day I discovered that the word 'baroque' translates roughly to: 'imperfect pearl, roughness'.

The week before, after a dinner with a journalist friend, a woman who calls herself a 'Brit-born Jamaican' sat back and told me that her paper has asked her to write Obama's obituary.

She explained that they like to have obituaries filed away as early as possible.

They update them on a regular basis.

We both shook our heads. This was an assignment that she had to turn down.

That's too much ju-ju.

I tell this to Duke and he laughs.

He says that she sounds like 'Miss Mildred', Queen of the Ruby Avenue Summer Party.

'Miss Mildred'.

After taking her 'little nip' of bourbon and branch water she would make sure that her favourite record came on: Chicagoan Phil Upchurch's *I Can't Sit Down*. She was totally obsessed with its good-time, jump-up feel. Her own child had been in military service with Upchurch and 'Miss Mildred' had met him from time to time. She liked his cheeky looks and bass guitar.

For her, it was like being back home, sitting on the porch, talking and laughing with people, forgetting all of the bad things beyond that road that stretched in front of your house.

To her mind, Upchurch was part of that happy time of people born in the South and who knew nothing of what really lay before them 'Up North'.

It was funny to watch our parents wiggle their hips and twist the night away to what Upchurch could conjure.

Even though he was younger than them, he knew something of their nostalgia and their need.

He came to understand our needs too, when, years later, he released a disc called *Darkness, Darkness*.

Even in that, the jaunty guitar was there, but it was muted, reflecting the horrors of those soldiers, serving and former, who had made it their anthem.

Darkness, Darkness is the other side of Marvin Gaye's epic *What's Going On?* and its rage in the night. *Darkness, Darkness* is the man who gets up in the morning, punches the clock, does his nine to five, goes home, and gets high all by himself so that he can do it all over again.

Figure it out all over again.

Upchurch reflected our parents' dreams, and the possibility of return.

But there was no possibility.

Not for us.

Unlike them, we did not come from there.

Between *I Can't Sit Down* and *Darkness, Darkness*, I took the lie and the lye out of my hair and went to cultural places like the Affro Arts Theatre.

I sat on the edge of things, but I understood that I had to be there.

Then, in the mid '60's, I began to see that our relatively gentle life in Ruby Avenue was being lived within an enclave – and that every breathing moment I had was bound up in the reality of my gender and the colour of my skin.

I discovered Von Freeman and his up and coming son Chico, smashing down walls with their tenor saxes. The Freemans are kings of 'outside' and there is something about 'outside' that is essential to what is made in this music scene, to tradition in Chicago.

All the while I was forging an identity through the activities at the South Side's Affro Arts, and listening to the music.

The jazz band The Pharaohs, with their dynamic drummer Maurice White who went on to be a founder and lead singer of

'Earth, Wind, and Fire', played there.

The Pharaohs were black Jews and black Muslims, playing together, making music that defined our youth and our greed to push the boundaries.

There was for us, too, the silver trumpet of Phil Coran and the Artistic Heritage Ensemble, who sured us up when we decided to wear our African garb in seriousness, and not as part of a fancy dress party.

When we corn-rowed our hair, put dozens of holes in our ears and tried to look like the Africa that was in our minds, there was Phil Coran to steer us, take away the gauze, see the work we had to do.

The movement that centered itself at Affro Arts was the continuation, by another name, of what had been built on the South Side, what had rooted itself there and what was growing still.

The South Side had taken the fortress built around it by segregation, changed it, and in many cases made it work. For us.

This doesn't make the fortress good, but it tells a story of human ingenuity, human faith.

And it was the music that gave us the call and a meaning for that call, so that we did what we did. Our way.

The music helped us to take the gangs and sit them down for a minute – see what we could do for ourselves and not against ourselves.

One evening, while I was working at the blues club on the North side, the Art Ensemble of Chicago trooped onstage.

Some of them were painted in African masks. I couldn't take my eyes off them.

They played.

At first it sounded as if all of the glassware on the bar had crashed at one point.

I wasn't sure that I could take it much longer, until, suddenly, I could hear it. The music. It was challenging and sublime.

They finished the set with a pristine rendition of something in classic Chicago Dixie-land style, paying homage to the sound that Chicago took from the riverboats ploughing the Mississippi and made its own, demonstrating that they could not only play their instruments superbly, but that what they played, they had chosen to.

The Art Ensemble re-invented the black experience, and rendered it into music.

The Art Ensemble of Chicago, broke another of jazz's ancient taboos. The music of The Art Ensemble was funny.

The Art Ensemble's patented 'little instruments' brought them fame.

Used them to 'create texture,' they often became tools for a playful and fun performance. They would take five hundred 'little instruments', for example, with them to concerts, including bike horns, kazoos, gongs, cymbals, ratchets, sirens maracas.

When they toured France, they took two tons of instruments with them.

South Siders wanted to break away from what they saw as the hierarchy of New York. They wanted to mix into jazz what they saw as South Side spontaneity, self-reliance and the South Side's drive to be the best.

This Movement's roots lie with The Experimental Band.

The Band began in the early sixties around the pianist Muhal Richard Abrams and other South Side musicians like Jack DeJohnette who often played with Miles Davis and John Coltrane. He also invited a few students from the local junior college who just wanted to play: Joseph Jarman, Roscoe Mitchell, Henry Threadgill.

Chicago music stations had switched largely to rock, and jazz musicians got less air play. Muhal Richard Abrams did a very South Side thing: he made this into an opportunity, and invited his friends to simply play the way that they wanted.

Abrahams guided the younger members to look at the times that they lived in, the immense civil rights changes, the changes in art, and fashion, but most of all, he led them to pursue things that mattered to them, what had brought them into the music.

Of course, they loved Coltrane. Coltrane, 'trane had gone off on his own journey of exploration, had set forth to walk on his own path.

The musicians around Abrams wanted to be playful, to open up the dialogue, the conversation.

Density, spontaneity, playfulness became a mark of this new 'Chicago School'.

The 'Chicago School' was about 'blowing out' – the exertion of robust energy – in order to use tradition to break tradition. My brother once saw one of the Art Ensemble's members play his instrument accompanied by a live cannon, shooting it off in one of the South Side's local parks.

Unlike the New York scene which could insist on the precise playing of an instrument as well as a rigid education in the canon, the 'Chicago School' relied on freedom within the group – just as Michelle Obama described as the beauty of a jazz ensemble.

And when soul singer Fomtella Bass, of *Rescue Me* fame, found a home and a husband within the Ensemble, she travelled to Paris with her celebrated spouse, Lester Bowie, this was the spirit of South Side jazz at its best – 'straight ahead.'

Move forward, while remembering, honouring, working with tradition.

Anthony Braxton, one of the original members of the Art Ensemble once stated that 'some of the most creative people I've met are not involved in music. They're simply living what the music is about.'

The South Side continued to nurture, groom, and allow to grow a kind of power. A power which could build until it could propel someone it had taken in, sheltered, fed, and send him along the long walk to the Capitol.

Richard Muhal Abrams made the following proposition to his South Side gathering:

What they were making was what he would call: *Great Black Music. Ancient to The Future.*

Frank

Waikiki.

In the Hawaiian language, the name means 'spouting fresh water.'

The young Barack Obama has driven from his grandparents' home to Waikiki for refreshment, for clarity.

For refuge.

He pours himself a whiskey at the house of an black poet who sometimes plays bridge with his grandfather, Stanley.

Stanley and Frank had grown up not far from one another back in Wichita, Kansas. But they would not have known one another.

Obama's grandfather, being white, would not have known Frank.

Indeed Frank has told Obama once, that back in the day, if Stanley had been walking along the pavement, he, Frank, would have had to yield and step into the road so that Stanley could pass.

He himself had come to Hawaii, not for the reasons Stanley had – to better himself – but to escape the madness that would have enveloped him and his white wife and their children at the end of the '40's.

Hawaii had a mixture of people of all colours, all living in relative harmony together. He had a half-white child, and Stanley had a half-black grandson, and they were both from Kansas, so, in Hawaii, their knowing one another made a bit of sense.

But Obama must not be confused. Frank had pointed out time and time again.

He and Stanley Dunham came from different worlds.

Barack has come to Frank's house because his beloved grandfather has just told him something that has shaken him to the core. His grandmother had been harassed at their local bus stop by a guy looking for handouts. He had frightened her. Because he was black.

Shaken by this emphasis on the colour of the man's skin, by his own flesh and blood, by people who had sacrificed everything for his education, Obama had felt himself enter a void. He had had to temporarily leave the house, find somewhere else to be.

Find an older black man to talk to.

The old poet is sanguine, laid back.

Stanley, the poet tells him, can't help himself, nor can his grandmother. That's the way they were raised, that's the way they were all brought up. That's why he himself came to Waikiki, to have a life of sorts.

Obama is listening to Frank. He knows that if his father's other sons – his Kenyan brothers – had come up to his grandmother, she would have recoiled in fear.

Those brothers were his flesh and blood as much as his grandparents were. But they were divided.

And within that divide is where he resides.

Obama, in recounting this episode in *Dreams,* writes that at that moment, sitting with the man who he later came to call 'old dashiki-wearin' Frank', he felt utterly alone.

It is accepted now by most sources that 'Frank' was the black American poet and author Frank Marshall Davis.

In his own unpublished memoirs, he mentions neither Stanley Dunham, nor Barack Obama.

It is said that in 1911, a group of white third graders, who had been told by their parents about lynching blacks, had sought out their black playmate and had tried to do the same thing to him. Just for fun.

At university he started writing poetry, and at the end of the twenties, he moved to Chicago where he worked for several of the thriving black newspapers at the time. There he wrote his first long poem: *Chicago's Congo: Sonata For an Orchestra*.

'I'm a grown-up man today in Chicago/ My bones are thick and stout/ (when I move to new districts bombings/ couldn't break them)/ My flesh is smooth and firm/ (look – the wounds you give me heal quickly)/ See how the muscles ripple under my/ (night-black skin/ You should be proud of me Chicago'…

After returning to Chicago in the '30's, following a spell in Atlanta, he became head of the ANP – Associate Negro Press, a powerful news service which sent out the news of the black community, and news of interest to the black community, all over America and the world.

Chicago contained the most powerful consortium of black news and publications in the world.

Davis started a photography club, and was encouraged to continue writing by none other than Richard Wright.

He started community organising and published a newspaper for workers in which he covered issues of racism.

He taught one of the first jazz history courses in the US.

Paul Robeson urged him to leave the mainland United States at the beginning of the anti-Left/anti-socialist/anti-Communist 'witchhunts' which began at the end of the '40's. Davis' commentaries on race, literature and American culture pointed to how that culture emerged from all of the elements that make up American society.

In the years that Obama knew him, Frank had become, on the island, an object of curiosity.

He had by then written a soft-core porn novel under a pseudonym which seems more like an act of provocation than anything else.

He is slowly being re-evaluated, not least because those in the anti-Obama camp point to Frank as having a great deal of influence over the young Obama, which those in defence of the President vehemently deny.

Yet, in *Dreams* the President recounts, during the days when he was community organising and wondering how he could best help the people of the South Side that: 'I imagined Frank in a baggy suit and wide lapels, standing in front of the old Regal Theatre, waiting to see Duke or Ella emerge from a gig.

And Frank dreamt of the South Side too, always.

In 1948 he published a book about life on the South Side: *47th Street: Poems*.

In a review of the time, the poems are described as detailing the end of the journey from the Deep South for the city's black people: 'hemmed in by restrictive covenants'. The South Side as 'the home of steel and stockyard workers', 'numbers' bankers (i.e. 'policy' – the black lottery run by and within the community which provided the only bank most people could use); the home of kitchenette dwellers, and mansion house roomers.'

Frank writes in *Livin' The Blues*: 'By contrast with the raw, savage strength of Chicago, I looked upon New York as a slick sissy, although I have never been there... I did not identify with those I considered Eastern writers…(on the South Side) there was no contact with white writers…our worlds were still separate…this lack of communication…fired my ambition to do for the Windy City what others had done in Harlem…if ever I became known, I intended it to be for my portraits of the South Side.'

Davis died in the '80's, not knowing that old Kansas Frank's black grandson would put the South Side on the map in a way he could never have dreamt of.

Self-knowledge was all to Frank Marshall Davis.

Prepare To Do Something Else

Late July, 2009.
The Grand Canyon.
Park Ranger, Scott Kraynak is giving the 'First Family' a tour.

They have followed a rail whose rim is a straight drop of 5,000 feet.

The First Family are in a long conversation with the ranger.

The President asks his eldest daughter to explain a bit about the type of rock to be found in the Grand Canyon.

She does so fluently and the ranger is impressed.

He comes back with the information that their beloved Chicago was once under water and that some of its buildings are made out of rock which was once coral reef.

And then the official photo.

Yet another picture of this family's back to us.

I have never seen so many images of a First Family shot from behind.

Is it to show their closeness, their solidarity, their up-against-the-world quality? In these photos the President always looks cocooned, almost hidden within his circle of women.

Are they meant to illustrate what the president said at a fund raiser: "I'm from Chicago. I don't break!"

Or are the pictures taken from behind telling us that this family is of themselves, moving away from us, leaving us?

These pictures have, for me, a haunting, sweet kind of dissonance, like the music of a South Sider I admire very much.

At the beginning of the '70's, when I met him, Henry was with the dancer-choreographer Christina Jones, one of the founding members of Jawole Willa Jo Zollar's 'Urban Bush Women', a ground-breaking black women's dance troupe whose members also spoke on stage, an unheard of thing for a dancer to do at the time. They had a delightful daughter by the name of Pyeng who is now a celebrated soul and jazz singer-musician in her own right.

Henry was part of the Art Ensemble of Chicago.

Of course, all of us highschoolers knew about Henry and the rest of band, but I didn't meet him until after he had returned from service in Vietnam.

He was one of that contingent of black soldiers who had met rock and roll head-on in the jungles of Southeast Asia and had responded by forming his own rock band while under arms.

That he had returned from that hell to continue making music was astounding.

Not everyone returned so well.

Larry from around the corner was deep into the avant garde jazz scene when we thought avant garde meant the lead singer of The Four Tops on Bernadette's imitation of Bob Dylan's over-arching talk/speak.

It was, after all, but Larry had gone much further.

Larry had gone to the 'Nam, because his test scores had not been good enough to get him into university.

When he returned sound of body, but not mind, we would steer clear of his solitary moods and musings on his mother's front steps.

He would blow smoke rings for hours at a time, watching them dissolve in the air and sometimes laughing like a little kid.

He would occasionally vanish, and then show up again without a word.

His mother got used to it. She had to.

Once he told me about 'the tripping bush' where he and his fellow soldiers would go to get high while they spent months underground waiting for a fight.

They had no idea that the Viet cong lived just below them in well-run compounds with hospitals, etc, something they had taken from the *Siege of Stalingrad* playbook of World War Two.

In the 'tripping bush', Larry said, you could get every kind of drug, and revel in the making of futile plots to 'frag' your senior officer, watch him explode into pieces, and then escape to some-place where the girls were nice and the booze and drugs were plentiful.

Obama has written that he is very attached to the '60's, that he knows what the decade was all about, even though he was a baby and little boy for all of it.

He attributes this to his mother who had given him a kind of template rooted in that time.

Henry Threadgill took that sound – the music that Larry could not express but which was in him – and extended it. Changed it.

Just as the President is attempting to do with the nation.

Henry Threadgill's music is very South Side – ensconced in the blues, gospel, soul and jazz – yet he abstracts them, pulls them as far as he can, stretches them, and in doing so creates something else.

It is the act of taking what is essentially abstract – that music created by the enslaved – and making it concrete.

Because of slavery, its strictures and cruelty, the real lives of the enslaved were invisible. The music is a manifestation of that invisible life, a kind of code and guide to it.

Just as President Obama, by his very being, extends the imaginative space of the Oval House, makes it impossible to not imagine his like ever there again, Henry takes all of what Muhal Richard Abrams called 'Great Black Music' and subtlety makes this adventurous music seem as if we had always heard it, always lived it.

This is called '*avant-garde*' and it is to most ears.

But it is 'regular', it is South Side.

Larry married a wonderful Jewish girl who loved him to pieces and gave him a lovely son.

For a time Larry was fine, holding down a job, bringing his paycheck home, coming back at night.

We would run into one another on Ruby Avenue, two fugitives back to our roots, two exiles from our origins: our clothing, our hair, our choice of companions foreign and odd, strangers now to the conventions in which we were raised.

But the 'tripping bush' and life in the tunnel summoned him into a void from which he refused to return.

He started sleeping rough about the time that Henry moved to the Lower East Side.

Henry went on to greater heights with his group 'Air', and other collaborations and groups, while Larry became one of those old vets who greet you at street corners with a paper cup for coins in one hand and a tale to tell in the other.

His wife begged me to look for him. The guy I had grown up

with had vanished into a pile of urine-soaked rags huddled over a heating grill in the middle of some busy street in the Loop.

One day he will end up in the Veterans Hospital; seeking his right to free medical care for his various ailments real and imagined.

Larry's cousin Jazel, also a friend, moved to Paris not long after Larry had gone off the rails.

His children are bi-lingual, but because of the way Larry turned out, and a few other things that he does not talk about, Jazel won't touch the US with a ten foot pole, but he makes sure that his passport is in tip top shape.

Jazel showed me once a poem that he had sent Larry, an excerpt from Rimbaud's *A Season In Hell*: '*Les blancs debarquant/ Le canon!/Il faut se soumetter au bateme, s'habiller, travailler.*' ('The whites are landing/The canon!/We must submit to baptism, put on clothes, work.)'

I have never forgotten it.

Jazel had come to Paris thinking quite simply that it was a less racist place to live. Because he could not speak French, his community was restricted to his fellow expats and he knew nothing of the black or the Arab world outside his door.

He didn't even see them. He walked around in a cloud like the rest of his circle, some kind of black version of Hemingway's *A Moveable Feast* playing on continuous loop in his head.

My first time in Paris, Jazel took me to Shakespeare and co. the bookshop on the Left Bank where we could read the latest books from the States and see who was in town.

The owner, an American World War Two vet by the name of George Whitman, presided at the cash register, and when I first entered that shop, there was a bouncy, funny blonde toddler running about.

She was George's daughter, Sylvia Beach Whitman, named after Sylvia Beach, the owner of the original Shakespeare and Co. some streets away.

There were lots of black male poets and musicians and writers there, and Sylvia was easy and a joy with them, particularly Ted Joans, whose work we heard one night after having far too much to drink.

After that we went somewhere and talked all night about the possibility of Jesse Jackson running for President.

It was the '80's and it was time.

But then we saw what he would go on to do as nothing more than a useful exercise, one doomed to failure.

We had been steeped in the works of Richard Wright and James Baldwin. They spoke truth to us, and we decided that we would never see the day that a black man put his hand on that Bible to take the Oath of Allegiance.

A decade or so later, Jazel sent me an email to tell me that Professor Henry Louis Gates was lecturing in London and I'd better go and see him.

So I sat in a sold-out auditorium at the Royal Festival Hall listening to Professor Gates speak.

I don't remember now what the theme was, but I do recall him saying something like: "Richard Wright was wrong."

And then, it seemed to me, he went on to put down Wright and James Baldwin, my literary heroes.

Richard Wright had written that Depression-era classic of South Side life: *Native Son*; and his autobiography *Black Boy* was so graphic about his life in Mississippi, the same sort of life my father would have lived, that I cannot to this day read it again.

James Baldwin quite simply echoed my own inner life, my own questions and searching and yearning to be more than the prisoner of my skin colour, my gender and my nation.

I ask Professor Gates what he thinks of ex-pats.

He replies to me that the 'people' will judge me if I have run away to write my own version of An *Ode to A Grecian Urn*.

Afterwards, a mutual friend comes over and says that Professor Gates would like me to join him for a drink.

Instead, I stand on Waterloo Bridge, gazing at the same Thames my father saw twice in his life and ask myself if the good Professor was right.

Had I run away? And would the South Side judge me for not staying, not fighting, not enduring?

On one hand Professor Gates is right.

I've met those ex-pats who have run away, who have changed their names, their accents, who simply don't want to know.

But there are those of us who take to heart that refrain from the gospel song: 'I got shoes/you got shoes/All God's chillun' got shoes.'

The fact that my ancestors and Professor Gates ancestors were bound to the land, locked in ghettos in the city, makes venturing out an act of defiance, not escape.

Being away allows us to see something else and bring it back home.

And the music of the South Side, that has touched and changed so much of the world, did not limit itself to the South Side.

So why should we?

The President spent part of his childhood 'abroad' – 'overseas' – and he gets the value of living elsewhere, of going further.

As Henry Threadgill, avant-garde South Sider, replied, when

asked how he would respond to music he had heard before; to a tune played by someone else; to music already in the world: 'I'd prepare to do something else.'

Obama Music

2009.
At the beginning of the Obama Presidency.
Michelle Obama, the First Lady, is visiting a classroom of what looks like First Graders – six and seven year olds.

She is talking to them, reading to them.

A little black guy stops her.

He asks: "Where is Obama?"

The First Lady replies that he is in the White House at work.

The little boy persists: "Where is Obama?"

The adults laugh, but the question lingers in the air.

Rome.
Early summer '09.
Poor Malia.

The British press has already dubbed her a 'Tween Queen' along with the barely-out-of-infancy Suri Cruise, and the rather long in the tooth for this designation Miley Cyrus.

Malia is dressed in a long t-shirt with a '60's peace sign on it, jeans, a pair of sunglasses perched on the end of her nose.

A very South Side going-to-the-mall look but the press has conjured up an entire article about it and God knows what else is in store for this kid and for her sister, too, as they go through life.

She is walking along the bottom of the Spanish Steps.

I want to tell her that if she stands at the top, there is a way to see straight to the beginning of the Vatican. A good, clean, straight Roman road, like Oxford Street or Bayswater Road.

And there is Sasha, cheery-take-it-all-in-her-stride.

I can see Sasha as a very old lady, like something out of the movie *Little Big Man* – a very, very old, wizened woman telling rather bored 22nd Century kids what it was like to have a daddy who was the first black President.

If this Presidency is to mean anything it has to mean that this very fact will be ancient history, like something from a faraway land that you can't quite believe.

It has to mean that the two Obama girls can proceed through life as human beings – very celebrated ones – but judged, in the end, by what Martin Luther King hoped for: 'the content of their character'.

I wish this for the babies of my nieces and nephews, none of them look at all related to me, with their pale skin and straight hair, but they are my direct descendants, just as my blue-eyed grandfather was my ancestor, that all this colour thing will mean nothing, nothing at all because black people; Black people; African American people; are and have always been a rainbow nation and always will be.

McCain and Clinton did not fully understand the world that they were in, that they hoped to run.

Clinton ran her famous '3a.m' ad, a masterpiece in unconscious paranoia and the unspoken, in which the implied question was: 'Would you want this inexperienced person to be on the other end of that hotline when the Big One is called in?'

What she didn't quite understand was that people wanted a world in which the phone DID NOT ring at 3 a.m., a world of sanity and order and peace.

They wanted change.

But the cruellest of our deceptions is that we believe that we want change.

We don't.

Not really.

Just an adjustment here and there.

A bit of shifting of the scenery. New characters on the stage.

But change?

No.

Not really.

The end of August '09.

Chicago is shut down for the day.

It's called a 'reduced service day'.

No public services except police and fire.

The elderly will receive no home visits, new mothers no assistance.

The Mayor expects to save many millions of dollars and other cities are watching.

There are bumper stickers popping up that read: 'Don't blame me. I voted for McCain.'

The blogosphere is fired up: 'President Obama has betrayed Candidate Obama' screams one; 'The Right Wing is like the little kid crying on the plane. Nobody turns around and tells him to shut up'; ' You reward your soldiers, not the ones who fought against you. He's demoralizing his base big time'; 'Send the Repubs a copy of 'Who Moved My Cheese' and let's leave 'em in the dust'; ' a lot of white folks were disgusted enough to stay home on Voting Day but not driven to vote for Obama.'; 'there's a counter-insurgency coming…'

And on tv is a prominent commentator, a former neo-con, pontificating.

I have to laugh and shake my head at all of the neo-cons who were shrill cheerleaders for Bush and Blair's war and who are now such manic Obama supporters.

I've had my conversion too, from Clinton to sceptic to Obama enthusiast, but I must have been on the fork just off the main road to Damascus where most of the neo-cons got struck blind, saw the light, and started dictating to the rest of us. Again..

Maybe I just couldn't get on it right away because it was so crowded.

Obama has grounded himself firmly within the people from whom he has chosen to emerge.

He has made himself through force of will, discipline and desire, he is part of the warp and woof of the institutions of the South Side.

He has married a formidable woman who comes out of the traditions that have allowed the South Side to survive and to rise again and again.

And as he said, Barack Obama does not break.

Neither does the South Side.

We are witnessing the 'Last Great Man' in the West.

He is this by virtue of the power that he wields.

And he is the last because we ourselves have moved on.

We no longer need the great orator who can sway us with words and vision.

Because – with all of our technology, machines that are growing faster than we are in brain power – we, the people, are becoming our own power, through the internet; but also through real-time, on-the ground activities such as single issue community organising. And we have yet to fully experience the power that partisan news broadcasting is becoming.

The People giveth. And the People taketh away.

In other words, Obama Music is our music, generated by us.

We have made this Presidency, we from the South Side, and everyone else who voted for and supports the 44th President of the United States.

This is what I hope:

That when his time as President is over under the Constitution, Barack Hussein Obama, who will only be in his mid fifties, will do this:

Return to his home on the South Side.

Kick off his shoes.

Sit back.

And listen to his own music.

And maybe this music might consist of what is contained in the words of Frank Marshall Grant, that old man, the Chicago poet, who took Barack in on Wakiki the night when the young future President of the United States realized that he was alone, singular, in this world:

'This song has no tune. You cannot hum it.

This song has no words, you cannot sing it.

This song everybody knows, nobody knows.'